WHAT CONFIDENT WOMEN DO

RACHEL STONE

Copyright © 2022 by Rachel Stone

All rights reserved.

No part of this book may be reproduced in any form or by any electronic or mechanical means, including information storage and retrieval systems, without written permission from the author, except for the use of brief quotations in a book review.

Claim Your Freebie NOW!

Get Good At Problem Solving

Want to know the secret behind getting good at problem solving? Everyone seems to be able to do it, but you're stuck in the pile of endless to-do lists with little progress.

Ok, so how do I get my FREE book?

EASY! See the next page

Claim Your Freebie NOW

Instructions:

1. Open the camera or the QR reader application on your smartphone.
2. Point your camera at the QR code to scan the QR code.
3. A notification will pop-up on screen.
4. Click on the notification to open the website link

Contents

Introduction ix

1. **HOW DO WE FEEL ABOUT BEING CONFIDENT?** 1
   Suzanne Lenglen 2
   Elizabeth Cady Stanton 4
   Do you know what it means to be confident? 5
   Consequences of lacking confidence 6
   What makes being confident a positive attribute? 7

2. **PASSIVE, ASSERTIVE, AND AGGRESSIVE COMMUNICATION STYLES** 9
   Why is self-assertion so difficult for me? 12

3. **BODY LANGUAGE** 14
   Acknowledging your personal body language 15
   Life-changing benefits of body language 18
   Using body language for your purpose 21

4. **HOW CONFIDENT WOMEN SPEAK** 24
   Why do we feel anxious being confident? 26
   Cognitive distortions caused by negative beliefs 30
   How to become a master of your own mind 31

5. **TAKE A BREAK - WHAT'S BEEN HOLDING YOU BACK?** 33
   Criticism and negative feedback 34
   Negative thoughts 34
   Anger 35
   Overthinking 37
   A sense of guilt 38
   Controlling your emotions 38

6. **DAILY ROUTINES FOR A CONFIDENT WOMAN** 41
   Identifying and addressing your desires 41
   Goal-setting 42

How to improve your habits	43
How to identify your boundaries	44

7. HOW CONFIDENT WOMEN ACT — 47
Examples of successful women — 48
Confident statements for different situations — 50
Learning to be confident in our relationships — 53
When your family doesn't appreciate your confidence. — 56
What should you do if your family ignores your assertiveness? — 57

8. CONFIDENT WOMEN IN THE WORKPLACE — 63
Asserting yourself as a worker — 64
Asserting yourself as a boss — 66
Knowing when and how to speak up for yourself — 68
How to defend yourself — 70

9. UNDERSTANDING HOW TO MANAGE DIFFERENT TYPES OF TREATMENT FROM OTHERS — 72
Dealing with aggression — 73
How to manage manipulation — 74
What to do when people make fun of you for being firm — 76
Asserting yourself may cause a lot of stress, so here's how you handle it — 77

Conclusion — 79
Feedback — 81

Introduction

Emotions are a natural part of the human condition. All of these aspects of our existence are connected. The way we express our emotions shows that we are sentient beings with a sense of control and influence over the world around us. Many individuals, on the other hand, seem to be emotionally unhinged. A captain who has lost command of his ship has lost control of his emotions when he loses control. The ship will go anywhere it wants, causing a lot of damage. A person's inability to manage his or her emotions will harm his or her relationships with others and his or her quality of life. The good thing about your emotions is that you can influence them. How effectively you can manage your emotions depends on how well you comprehend this fact.

We live in a world where everyone has so many expectations. Your workplace expects a lot from you. Many of life's difficult challenges, as well as professional assignments, may create stress and harm to our health. Everyone needs to avoid shifting the blame for their challenges on others when they feel threatened since this is an action that may hurt their lives. As you engage with people regularly, you are certain to face problems and learn from them. To master your emotions, you must first get a thorough understanding of them.

Being self-assured isn't something we learn at birth. It's tough to speak out for ourselves in daily settings when we have a timid attitude like this. Our mental and physical health deteriorates over time due to this gradual excessive wear. We can't go on living a life that is all about making other people happy when we're not happy ourselves.

Since you were a child, you've heard others say things like "You need to have greater self-confidence" or "Go achieve what you want." Anyone who suffers from a lack of assertiveness understands how difficult this is.

Many individuals attribute our lack of confidence in ourselves to a lack of intellect, whether practical or emotional. On the other hand, we are very intelligent, hard-working, and skilled. Despite this, individuals that know how to stand up for themselves tend to be the ones who garner the most attention.

On the other hand, we fear that our aggressiveness may hurt others. I was afraid of upsetting or disappointing others if I said no to their requests. Eventually, you stop loving your life and become resentful of being used as a tool by others. You may be forced to work longer hours or endure uncomfortable family meals. We can't reveal our actual feelings because we're afraid of what other people may think. We walk on eggshells for years at a time.

This book combines information, exercises, and tried-and-tested techniques that you can use right now to improve your life. Understanding some of our most common issues with assertiveness will be the focus of this class.

Our lack of confidence, fear of rejection, and shame keep us from being more forceful, according to our own experience. However, we're not going to play the blame game and point fingers at ourselves for why it's so hard to speak out for ourselves. Instead, we'll examine the psychological factors at play to find a solution.

It's not only in one aspect of our life that we feel the desire to express ourselves. As a result, time should be set aside to provide counsel that may be applied to various circumstances and types of relationships. It intrigues me how people behave differently, and I believe that learning more about human behaviour can help you make the necessary changes.

It doesn't matter how long or short you think your life is; it's here to be savoured. I desire that everyone who reads this book will begin to feel the pleasure in their life, whether it be in their work, personal relationships, or how they see the world around them.

We will learn how to create boundaries in our relationships so that saying no becomes easier. All people have a right to express their feelings and be happy, and this is what we want to do.

Assertiveness is something about which society today seems to be perplexed, giving us conflicting signals. We're advised to keep our thoughts to ourselves at once, and then we're encouraged to be pushy to achieve what we want the next.

The difficulty is that we have to learn to balance passive and aggressive behaviour on our own, and it's good to ask for guidance when you need it. It is, after all, a highly complex subject.

You've concluded that something has to be done if you're here. Let's have a better grasp of confidence in the first stage.

1

How do we feel about being confident?

WHEN WOMEN ARE STILL STRUGGLING for equal pay for equal (and sometimes—dare I say—better) work, it's simple to understand how our self-esteem may suffer. Remember, we're still getting over centuries of being taught to be seen but not heard, serving without being served. The outdated and "traditional" assumption that a woman's function is just to cook, clean, and smile in the living room has been fought back by contemporary feminism; now, we women confront work and leisure, motherhood and muscle, and beauty and bossiness. There is no higher attribute for the world's most successful CEOs and leaders than bossiness.

In addition, women have always had a strong sense of self-confidence. It's existed from the beginning of oppression itself. Think about women like Esther and Joan of Arc, both of whom walked with their shoulders back and their heads held high despite the lack of resources in their patriarchal communities. Do you think they didn't? And they aren't the only ones who have risen to the top despite being women. The longest-reigning British monarch, Queen Elizabeth II, is both female and still in power, yet the United Kingdom isn't the only sovereign state to have had a woman in command. A peaceful transfer of power in Liberia was made possible in 2018 when Ellen Johnson Sirleaf stepped down as Liberia's president, becoming Africa's first elected head of state. It's not only Ellen Johnson Sirleaf's role as a role model for African women who are taking up the helms of democracy; women in Rwanda make up almost half the country's parliament. From the pre-United States kingdom of Hawaii to Nigeria and Egypt, France and Spain, China, India, and Russia, women have reigned in a wide range of countries. They refused to be held back by the males (and even other women) who looked down on them.

On the other hand, confidence should not be reserved for the king or queen. Any woman may see her value, as you'll see from the diverse group of women who have been mentioned below. In the end, these ladies know who they are, and you can do the same. To be honest, no one should ever have to convince you that simply getting through in this world filled with hatred and violence is an achievement in and of itself. Everyone needs daily affirmations of their dignity to keep them motivated and focused on their goals. You are.

You're exactly like the woman in the following paragraphs. You're not going to bow down. You won't be forced to do anything you don't want to. You're not going to budge an inch. Deep down, we both know you're precisely who you should be.

Suzanne Lenglen

1899 saw the birth of a young woman named Suzanne in Paris. She was weak for much of her childhood and had several health issues, including asthma. According to her father, tennis would strengthen her and improve her health. In 1910, she made her first foray into tennis on the home court, and her father started to teach her how to compete. In 1914, at the age of fourteen, Lenglen reached the final of the French Championships (now the French Open), losing to Marguerite Broquedis. Still, she went on to win the World Hard Court Championships in Paris on her fifteenth birthday, making her the youngest person in tennis history to win a major championship.

After making her Wimbledon debut in 1919 against seven-time

winner Dorothea Douglass Chambers, Lenglen went on to win the tournament for the first time. King George V and Queen-Consort Mary of Teck were among the 8,000 spectators who saw the historic event. Lenglen prevailed, but it wasn't only her talent that attracted public attention. Other competitors participated in body-covering outfits, so the media was outraged by her clothing, which showed her forearms and stopped above the calf. This French woman-athlete dared to consume brandy between sets, which startled the reserved British.

Lenglen swept the women's singles tennis competition in Belgium at the 1920 Summer Olympics. Only four games were lost on the route to a gold medal, three of which were in the final versus Dorothy Holman of England. She earned a gold medal in the mixed doubles event; she was ousted in the quarterfinals of the women's doubles but gained bronze when the opposing team withdrew. From 1919 until 1925, she won the Wimbledon singles title every year except 1924, when she had to quit due to health issues after winning the semifinal. As a professional tennis player, Lenglen won six French Championship singles titles and five double crowns between 1920 and 1926. Incredibly, she only lost seven matches in her career.

When Suzanne Lenglen became a professional, she was the first major female tennis player to do so. Despite reaching the final of the French Championships the year before, Mary K. Browne fell to Lenglen and managed just one point in the match, which was funded by sports entrepreneur C. C. Pyle, who paid her $50,000 to play a series of matches against her. This was the first time that a women's match was the main event of a tour, even though male players were also present. As of early 1927, Lenglen had won all of her thirty-eight matches on tour, but her doctor suggested a long break from the sport. With the support of Jean Tillier, her longtime boyfriend, she chose to withdraw from tennis and open a tennis school. Aside from writing tennis books, Lenglen also expanded the school and made it known.

Lenglen's brilliance, energy, and flair had permanently altered women's tennis. She is widely believed to be one of the greatest tennis players of all time. In 1978, she was admitted into the International Tennis Hall of Fame. A trophy named "Coupe Suzanne Lenglen" was first awarded to the winner of the women's singles event at the French Open in the following year. As the world witnesses women's tennis brilliance, agility, and exhilaration, Suzanne Lenglen's legacy is being passed down from champion to champion.

Elizabeth Cady Stanton

The National Women's Suffrage Association was founded in 1869 by Susan B. Anthony and Elizabeth Cady Stanton also published a feminist newspaper called The Revolution.

It was Anthony and Cady Stanton who pushed for the inclusion of women's right to vote as soon as the 14th Amendment was ratified in 1872, giving all Americans "equal protection of the laws" and particularly preserving the voting rights of "any of the male residents" of any state. However, Congress disregarded the several amendments to women's suffrage presented each year, and women's voting rights didn't arrive until over fifty years later.

Neither Stanton nor Anthony was afraid to get their hands dirty. The first women's rights convention was founded in 1848, with a program promoting property rights, equal pay for equal labour, and the right to vote, with Stanton and Lucretia Mott as co-chairs. Later on, three years later, Stanton was introduced to Susan Anthony. Their "ideal team" combined Elizabeth's political ideas and her ability to arouse people's emotions with Susan's unequalled competence as a logician and organiser. To everyone's surprise, they created the first women's temperance association, and their request for the legal recognition of drunkenness as a reason for divorce shocked everyone.

It wasn't until after Elizabeth Cady Stanton's death that she was able to see this historic triumph come to fruition for the women of America. As a result of their historic first women's rights conference in 1848, only Charlotte Woodward survived to witness the passage of the 1920 amendment granting women the right to vote—the only one of 260 women present at the meeting.

It doesn't matter whether these women are better or worse than you in this regard. In reality, they don't differ in any way from you. You are just as talented, intelligent, and powerful as everyone else. Instead of putting yourself down, use these quotations to inspire you. To remind yourself of what women are capable of and what you are capable of. Also, to serve as a constant reminder that being self-assured is perfectly OK. Being self-assured is a virtue in and of itself. And you're entitled to it because you've earned it.

Your strength, independence, and beauty will serve you well in the present and the future. Reminding yourself of this will help you to accomplish more than you ever thought possible.

Do you know what it means to be confident?

Let's get things off to a good start. Confidence is often seen as a positive quality in individuals. Those who can express themselves inspire admiration and a desire in us to do the same. Because of our lack of self-belief, we believe we will never be able to accomplish our goals. Just like all of the other abilities you currently possess, confidence is a skill that can be learned.

It is necessary for persons who have people-pleasing inclinations to learn how to establish themselves to interact more effectively with their friends, family, and coworkers. Assertiveness is not a negative quality, and you no longer have to worry about how the other person will respond. It's a highly useful ability to possess.

Confident people don't feel guilty or nervous about acting in their own best interests. A substantial shift is required for individuals who have placed other people's needs and aspirations ahead of their own, but remember that you aren't doing anything out of the norm.

Let's look at an ordinary example of how confidence should and shouldn't appear.

Sam and Jason want to remodel their living room. Jason wants to paint it a dark blue, but Sam is afraid it will make the entire room appear too tiny. Alternatively, Sam may turn around and say, "That's a bad concept, and we're not going to implement it!" This might be seen as an aggressive tone. Despite Jason's objections, she refuses to listen to him.

This hasty remark is likely to irritate Jason, and it may even make him furious. When an event that should be thrilling turns into a full-blown dispute, you've probably experienced similar encounters.

With her assertive abilities, Sam may have calmly said that she was undecided and suggested they go to a paint shop for some samples. This might provide some new ideas and, perhaps, a solution.

In contrast, Jason would have been able to defuse the situation and yet get his point through if he had strong confidence.

It's easy to lose patience and come across as hostile when under constant stress. To avoid causing a stir, it may be more convenient to be a passive participant. While none of these extremes is desirable behaviour, both can be corrected with the proper information and skills when you have them.

Consequences of lacking confidence

Our focus here is not going to be on the bad aspects. If you're reading this, you're most likely acutely aware of your pain. In certain cases, you may need some help identifying that your issues arise from a lack of self-confidence.

Because of your lack of self-confidence, it may be difficult for you to speak out for yourself in certain situations. Fear of the repercussions of sticking up for oneself is a common motivation behind people-pleasing behaviour.

Putting our own needs and desires ahead of others might cause us to feel self-conscious. Because your buddy is busier than you, you should make arrangements around their availability. Isn't it selfish to want to accomplish something while you're free?

The lack of assertiveness might lead to a lack of collaboration. There is a sense of relief in the beginning that they always get their way, but this is not the case in a long-term relationship. Because one spouse was usually out with their buddies, I've seen many relationships fall apart. Their friends don't want to spend as much time with them as they would want. Their other relationships begin to suffer due to their obligation to do so.

In certain cases, individuals cannot express themselves due to a strong feeling of responsibility or commitment to others. Today's era of instant access to information and communication means that we are seeing an increase in the prevalence of this phenomenon. We've lost the notion of a 9 to 5 job because we're expected to respond to emails and text messages as soon as they arrive. There are much more serious ramifications to this than we are aware of, and this is contributing to 'Work Stress.' To avoid becoming a slave to our smartphones, we have become too kind to say no or set limits.

When this behaviour continues over an extended period, it may lead to feelings of worry and depression. There is a danger that we may fall into a pattern of unhealthful habits and actions. Some individuals resort to alcohol or drugs because they aren't getting enough food or sleep. I understand how demoralising this may be, particularly if your only goal in life is to be a nice person.

What makes being confident a positive attribute?

I've seen that confidence has gotten a poor rap over the years since individuals tend to overdo it and seem pushy. Assertiveness is a good way to communicate. In this chapter, we'll look at the advantages of confidence and how to practice it.

Allows you to do the following:

- Boost your self-esteem and self-confidence.
- Get a better handle on how you feel.
- Be respected.
- Improve your ability to communicate effectively.
- Find a middle ground in difficult circumstances.
- Decide more wisely.
- Become a part of real, open relationships.
- Reduce your level of stress.
- Get more out of your work and enjoy it more.

First, I had to understand that being assertive wasn't always a negative thing when done well. It may be nerve-wracking to examine our conduct and how others see us, and it's not a skill that can be learned in a day. To perceive these characteristics in ourselves, we must first examine the distinctions between passive, aggressive, and assertive conduct.

2

Passive, assertive, and aggressive communication styles

IN THE ABSENCE OF INSTRUCTION, it might seem like we're teetering on the edge of a precarious precipice. To seem forceful, you must walk a fine line between assertive and quiet.

As a general rule, people who find it difficult to exert themselves tend to be on the more docile end of the scale. We seldom go over the line since our first concern is for the well-being of others rather than our own needs.

What qualifies as passive?

The need to be liked and the inability to perceive oneself as equal to others are the root causes of passivity. There is little value in their goals, dreams, and ambitions compared to others. When individuals don't perceive the value of expressing their views and opinions, they tend to avoid expressing their thoughts and opinions out of fear that they won't be taken seriously.

Being passive implies that other people are more inclined to make choices for you, which is a purposeful act. Your life may seem out of your control because of this. The final consequence is that your love life is dictated by your friends and family, even if it seems like a joke.

Even though they are overworked, passive people have difficulty saying no when asked to do anything. The other person will not be able to tell that their answer implies that they have no time. When their wish is granted, they only hear about it.

Let us consider how a passive individual might respond to the inquiry, "Can you make dinner tonight?"

How would they respond? "Well, I was expecting to order Chinese tonight and watch a DVD since I am tired, but if I go to the shop, I can cook an Indian curry meal."

They wanted nothing more than to end a hard day at work, curl up on the couch, and take a breather. They have considered the other person's needs and prioritised this above their own. The passive person will go to great lengths to make the other person happy. "I won't be able to tonight because I'm exhausted," might be a more assertive statement. "I can do it tomorrow."

An important distinction between the two responses is that a confident person has taken the time to assess if they can prepare dinner and have answered based on their own needs and other commitments.

When you're a passive person, you run the danger of others discovering that you're unwilling to say no. It doesn't matter whether you're dealing with this at work or in your personal life; it won't suddenly end. As a result, you end yourself doing things you'd rather not or can't do yourself.

What qualities make someone aggressive?

Aggressive conduct may be restricted to situations in which a person's anger or voice is raised. There may be even more steps involved. Interruption, ignoring someone, or telling someone what to do instead of asking are all examples of rude behaviour.

Aggressive conduct might leave you feeling upset, confused, or even afraid. When someone reacts negatively toward you, you may wonder whether there is anything wrong with you that caused this to happen in the first place.

Unfortunately, since the message is often muddled, aggression often results in a breakdown in interpersonal communication. You may just hear the person's aggravation and anger, not what they're trying to express.

An aggressive person cannot give credit to others for their efforts when they have done something effectively. The chances of receiving a thank you are little to none. They will not appreciate your efforts to grant their requests since they don't have the time. Humour and sarcasm are sometimes taken for what they are not—another type of hostility.

Sam's reaction was forceful, as we witnessed with her and Jason. However, to have a fruitful dialogue, we must examine all sides. Jason may be able to exert his authority. Alternatively, he may respond in a way that confuses Sam by being aggressive or quiet.

As we go through the book, we'll take a deeper look at how to distinguish passive and aggressive conduct and discover your equilibrium.

Mixed messages.

Passive-aggressive conduct is something you may have heard about a lot, and it may lead to a lot of bad sentiments and thoughts. The word "passive-aggressive" is often misinterpreted because it is frequently misunderstood. This is compounded by the fact that things may become a little murky in terms of culture.

Inaction, when a response is anticipated, is a rough definition of passive-aggressive conduct. Examples of passive-aggressive behaviour include tardiness, intentionally forgetting things, and underperformance. In the workplace, this kind of conduct is widespread, and it may be because the individual cannot articulate their feelings.

We may become passive-aggressive because we want to say no, but we keep saying yes. We might acquire a bad attitude since it is difficult to express our feelings in words.

It's a sign of passive-aggressive behaviour if your supervisor refuses to answer your questions. This is unfair to you, given your inability to do your duties. The unclear element comes from the fact that sarcasm is also a kind of passive-aggressive conduct. Sarcasm may be funny at times, and this is what we term passive-aggressive conduct. Satirical sarcasm is referred to as passive-aggressive conduct when it persists over an extended period.

Passive-aggressive conduct is now known as covert aggression, and dealing with it is a major part of what we'll be studying. A person's ability to subtly assert one's will is "covert aggressiveness." Subtly aggressive people will try to manipulate and exploit you somehow, whether by telling you lies, making you feel like a victim, or feeling guilty.

Like violence, this is a behaviour that you are unlikely to engage in regularly. This isn't to argue that people who lack self-confidence can't be furious. I have often felt furious with myself and the world because of our insatiable urge to say yes to everything. As a people-pleaser, I'd never show this part of myself to others.

Why is self-assertion so difficult for me?

Remember that no one is to blame here. Each person can identify with one or more of the following reasons: If you're not interested in going into your fear of assertiveness, you can start developing the skills you need right now. That makes sense to me. When you graduate from high school and enrol in college, you are essentially an adult, but you are still susceptible to social pressures that tell you what is right or wrong. We are bombarded with messages that encourage us to ask for what we want, and then the next week, we are instructed to go out and get it. When confronted with this decision, I'm torn between asking and accepting. Do I stand up for myself?

The reasons individuals give for not being able to speak out for themselves are amazing, and we can learn a lot from them. The guilt of putting yourself first or the fear of hurting someone else's emotions are just a few of our previously discussed issues. Worse, there's the worry that you won't be loved by or get the approval of someone.

In contrast to a cold or the flu, a lack of self-confidence is not contagious. It's not something you can simply get one day. This is a habit that you may have picked up as early as your early years of life. Making a child's parents pleased is only natural. As long as they get praise and affection for their positive conduct, they'll keep going in that direction. As a result, the anxiety of being rejected develops. Everyone around us should be pleased, and we should not be penalised for our actions. This, on its own, is probably insufficient.

We only begin to notice an issue when other elements are brought into play. The problem becomes more problematic when you add a timid personality to the mix. It's possible to lose your self-confidence to the point where you don't express yourself.

In a poor relationship, you may have learned that your ideas don't matter and your needs aren't important. Emotional anguish or trauma, such as the death of a loved one, divorce, or physical violence, may also lead to depression.

Putting a label on something we're afraid of or worried about won't make it disappear. When you acknowledge your fear of rejection, it doesn't mean you'll be able to manage it. I think it's a touch too basic for psychology's complexity. On the other hand, understanding why you are afraid to be assertive can help you discover the strategies that will be most effective for you in the long run.

Before we discuss coping with our negative emotions, I want you to step back and study yourself. Spend a day or two observing individuals in various settings to discover how they make their opinions heard. Your parents, co-workers, friends, or anybody else might be the source of your stress.

3

Body language

WE WANT to get to the heart of what our closest friends and family members say when we speak to them. Our goal is to avoid missing a vital piece of information if they are discussing a challenging subject. Whenever we're having a serious conversation with our spouse, we don't want to miss a sign that they're not happy with our words. As a parent, we want to make sure that our joy over a child's performance on a sports team resonates with them.

These are all things to keep an eye out for a while having a discussion. It's impossible to convey all of these intricacies in words alone. Whether we like it or not, our bodies will always be there to help us talk about and convey our feelings. Body language helps us understand each other better in our talks. This degree of awareness is only possible if you can interpret body language and put what you've learned to good use in your interactions and relationships.

Things aren't always what they seem to be when it comes to this issue. If someone tells you they love you and their face isn't smiling, you could assume they're lying. They may be exhausted in actuality. Many people communicate more with their facial expressions than their words, even if this example may seem apparent.

In addition, if you speak one thing while feeling another, your body may be telling the truth about your emotions. Many people declare they love someone yet cannot look them in the eye. Indeed, you may see people lowering their gazes while they say this. This might be a sign of surrender, but it could also be a clue that they lie.

It is evident from this example that your body language impacts the individuals around you. Your body language may indicate that you are telling the truth or telling a lie. Using your body language to convey a range of emotions might also help them understand how you're feeling at the moment. Your body language is usually a good indicator of how you feel about the individuals you're speaking to. They'll be able to read right through your words to your true feelings if they can pick up on these signs.

Acknowledging your personal body language

Having the ability to interpret body language isn't only beneficial to others, but it's also crucial to understand your body language. It might be challenging to see oneself from a third-party viewpoint since it's not always simple to perceive yourself that way. To help you better understand yourself, I suggested that you check in with yourself in a mirror or even on camera.

Your body language can only be deciphered if you can keep a close eye on your movements. Observe the tiniest shifts in your body, such as the smallest movement of your shoulders or legs. Even the motions your body does not make in a certain setting need your attention. For example, you could avoid eye contact, which can make a discussion seem unpleasant.

Self-awareness of one's body language might be a challenge, but it is an extremely valuable talent to have at one's disposal. Here, we'll look at what your body language can be telling others. As a result, you'll be able to communicate more effectively by aligning your words and actions.

What your body language could reveal about you.

One of the most common reasons people become interested in nonverbal communication reading is to figure out if someone is lying to them. No one is born with the ability to be a "human lie detector," as the term implies. Even though they are intelligent, they have mastered the art of reading people better than anyone else.

For example, they are well-versed in eye contact and eye movement. The lack of eye contact is a telltale sign of a liar. It is possible to detect lies even if someone deliberately avoids your gaze. Look for "shifty" eye movements in your interlocutor, which are movements from left to right of the eyes as if someone is following them. This involuntary movement of the eyes may signify that something is wrong.

Others may feel better about themselves because of your body language.

When it comes to communicating with others, your nonverbal cues can profoundly impact. If you touch the person, smile, laugh, and look at them more than normal, you may offer them precisely the boost of self-esteem they are seeking for. Of course, you have to be cautious with your touch since it may easily become creepy if it's done without your permission.

It's true that open gestures like putting your arms out while you talk, or even simple smiles, may go a long way toward making people feel more at ease with you. Behaving will show your opponent that you're receptive and ready for conversation.

"Mirroring" is another key factor to keep in mind. Being "in sync" with your interlocutor is acting similarly to how they do. As a result, your counterpart will begin to believe that you "understand" them on a subliminal level. We'll get into this in more depth later, but for now, you can just observe what the other person is doing and acting like.

Your body language may make other people angry.

Subtle acts that are the exact opposite of those described above may have the opposite impact. Keep your distance, don't grin or laugh with the person you're conversing with, or just don't pay much attention to them, and they may feel uncomfortable. The way you speak has a huge impact on how people feel about you, and your tone of voice is no exception. As a result, you should make an effort to ensure that your voice conveys your true feelings.

Your body language may be hard for people to understand.

The people around us may decipher our body language in various ways. If we stand close to them and smile at them, they will undoubtedly understand that we are enjoying our time with them and appreciate them for who they are. The person will pick up on our negative energy if we ignore them or speak to them without looking at them. There are times when your body language is inconsistent or does not match your feelings. This might be confusing to others.

A colleague who doesn't look at you while shaking your hand exemplifies this. What are your thoughts about that? Does this individual seem disinterested in you, or maybe hates you? A lack of eye contact might send the wrong impression if you've ever been in this circumstance.

On the other hand, what if you had a co-worker you hated but found yourself looking at and smiling regularly? If so, would it be an accurate depiction of your feelings? You may be simply being courteous to avoid offending the other person. However, you may unknowingly convey inconsistent signals since other components of your body language may reveal your genuine sentiments.

I remember when two co-workers who didn't like each other met at a conference. Professionalism and politeness were evident in both. Despite smiling and exchanging brief pleasantries, their discontent was painfully apparent when they offered one other a limp handshake. Things became a little weird very fast.

This means you must be conscious of your body language and ensure it fits your feelings and how you want to introduce yourself to others for your body language not to be misunderstood.

When it comes to the dating scene, your body language might give the wrong message. In the search for love, smooth-talking people typically have the appropriate game plan but often lack the nonverbal communication to complement it.

Smooth talkers may be adept at persuasion, but they often lack appropriate body language and often resort to creepy or cringe-inducing touching. Some so-called dating gurus advise their followers to touch the other person early and frequently send the message that they are interested in the other person.

To reiterate: uninvited touching may be weird straight away and undermine your chances of building a real connection with someone in seconds. Uninvited touching is creepy.

As a result, your appearance and demeanour should be a high priority. You'll have a far better opportunity of connecting with your interlocutor if you maintain a professional demeanour, smile naturally, and show consideration for their personal space.

Your body language can make you look confident.

Faces and gestures may give away a person's level of confidence or lack thereof only by their body language and facial expressions. Your attitude conveys your level of self-assurance. Confident people, for example, have a squared-off shoulder and a straight-ahead look. While sagging shoulders may only be a sign of poor posture, the truth is that your posture reveals considerably more than you realise.

You must be very aware of how you move and act if you want your body language to convey confidence. You must add strong body language motions into your daily routine. The ability to make even the tiniest of changes might be challenging, but once mastered, it can be quite useful.

As a general guideline, it's good to pay attention to your body language and make sure it matches your words. Ensure your body language reflects your words if you are really in love with someone. Make sure that your body language doesn't upset the person you dislike. In the end, politeness is not a bad thing at all.

Life-changing benefits of body language

We all know that body language may be highly helpful in your life. When you are conscious of your body motions, it might enable you to be portrayed in the manner you want others to see you. It can also tell you how the people in your immediate vicinity are feeling, which is really useful information.

The ability to understand body language is one of the first benefits you'll enjoy from mastering it. Observing someone's body language may help you learn more about their state of mind and help you reach out to them. You may have saved the person's life if they were too sad to seek your assistance, and you were able to pick up on their emotional signs. Consistent sobbing, a lack of eye contact, and a body posture that shows a loss of self-esteem are all things to watch out for in a scenario like this. In other cases, the individual may even be unable to normally move or engage in conversation. Maybe they're reclining in a way that isn't typical of them, or they're holding their head lower than usual. They may withdraw to the periphery of a group, acting as though they want to be by themselves. If you can recognise these acts and reach out to them from a support position, you may be able to aid them considerably in their challenges when they might otherwise not have gotten any help.

A person's body language may reveal more than just depression, and it's not just depression. In addition to social anxiety and GAD (Generalised Anxiety Disorder), panic attacks and other anxiety may also appear. Someone who is generally calm but is fidgeting or moving about excessively, such as wringing their hands or tapping their foot, may be experiencing anxiety about something they are presently doing or about something they will be doing in the future. You may have noticed a friend's posture as they stand, their arms folded in front of them and their chest thumping. This might be a telltale symptom of someone experiencing a panic attack since they are hyperventilating and attempting to shrink themselves as much as possible. When someone's body language shows anxiety, you may reach out to them in the same way you would to someone who is depressed and assist them in getting through the attack instead of leaving them to suffer alone.

Body language may also help you attract people's attention because you engage with them. When looking for new friendships or love partners or significant others, look at the recommendations we discussed in the last section on utilising your body language.

As indicated before, your body language may also protect you. As a warning sign, it might indicate that you will get into an altercation. It can tell you if someone isn't pleased with what you're saying. Change the topic if you see someone becoming agitated while speaking, lowering their chin and eyebrows, and breathing more deeply.

We may use body language to our advantage in the workplace. People will follow your example and pay attention to your words if you exhibit body language. Being able to convey self-assurance via your physical appearance may help you get the job of your dreams. Make eye contact, stand tall, and often smile to achieve this. If you keep your head up, others will see you the way you want them to.

Even if you're not comfortable expressing it out loud, you may be able to convey your dislike for something via body language. Even if you don't want to speak out when someone says anything that annoys or offends you, you may reduce your eye contact with them and lower your look. You might do this by placing your hands over your chest and lowering your chin to your chest as an alternative. You might also choose to stop smiling. Signs like this might help you make your idea clearer.

You may even use body language to persuade your colleagues to join you on a project. Make eye contact and employ body language that indicates you're interested in the activity, and others will follow your lead and join in the fun.

You may begin a discussion with a firm handshake if you want to get to know someone professionally. As a result, the other person will also begin to respect you.

Smiling is a simple way to lift the spirits of those around you. When you smile, others are more inclined to do the same. As a result, their bodies will also be filled with delight. Make someone's day brighter and your own with this simple gesture.

Your body language may improve even the way you speak and how others listen to you. Talking with your hands is an easy way to do this. This piques the curiosity of others in the room and gives the impression that you are a more experienced speaker.

Understanding body language may positively impact your life in several ways. Tips in this chapter may help improve your life in general.

Using body language for your purpose

Using body language to make friends is the first step. Being aware of your body language and the body language of others around you may be immensely beneficial if you often attend social gatherings but aren't making any new acquaintances.

Make an effort to seem approachable and eager to engage in conversation. Smile and create eye contact with the folks in your immediate vicinity. Also, make sure that your torso is open and your feet are shoulder-width apart as you stand.

For the next step, pay attention to how individuals around you are acting. If a person stands or sits with their head in their hands in searching for a new buddy, they are unlikely to be a suitable fit. You'll want to look for someone who uses body language comparable to your own.

When you've struck up a conversation with a stranger, employing your new mirroring talents is good. If you mimic their facial expressions and body language, you may be able to establish a rapport with the individual you're meeting. As a result, you may develop a new acquaintance in a manner that you never thought possible.

Using body language to discover a new love interest is the next step. Finding a new romantic partner is comparable to creating a new friend. Using the same body language techniques can help you look open and welcoming. In addition to the body language we have over for friendship, you will want to put in some romantic aspects. To make yourself seem more beautiful to the individuals you are conversing with, you may stand with your chest outward. Make eye contact with the individual and softly touch them while talking to demonstrate your attention. Laughing at their jokes is also a good way to indicate their interest.

If you want to succeed in the job, you need to learn how to read body language. When it comes to doing this, Power Stances are a useful resource. Confidence and trustworthiness are important qualities to project. Doing so will demonstrate your leadership abilities and earn you the respect of your peers and superiors.

Using your body language has numerous advantages, but you may also gain greatly from being able to interpret the body language of others who are around you.

You can easily determine whether someone is lying just on their body language. If you have any reason to believe the person you are speaking with is lying, you should pay attention to their body language. No, they're not touching their noses with their hands. Are they speaking with their mouths shut? If so, do they seem to be fidgeting and tapping their toes nervously? Signs that the person you're speaking with is lying might include any or all of the following. You can tell whether someone is dishonest just by looking away from you or if they're staring at you for a long time.

You may also utilise body language to your advantage by reading it and changing your own. If you and a buddy are out for drinks at a bar and a stranger approaches you while getting drinks, you could strike up a conversation with them. There is a noticeable shift in this person's body language as they begin to lean in closer to you, uncross their arms, place one knee on top of the other, and even dilate their eyes without any noticeable change in lighting. You've learned about body language in this book, and you think they're more interested in you than just friendship. If you don't feel the same way about them, you may let them know by changing your body language, which won't offend them. Avoid eye and physical contact with them by leaning away from them, crossing your arms over your chest, etc. We expect them to take the hint and move on. Your body language may also be manipulated to make it seem like you are more than just pals with your buddy. It is best to avoid displaying amorous body language to avoid a potential conflict. This ability to understand and use body language is especially useful for women.

Body language may one day be used as self-defence in a potentially harmful circumstance. Observing someone's body language might reveal whether or not they want to harm you in any other manner. Is their other hand holding their arm behind their back? There is the possibility that they are restrained from striking you. Is it a big huff on their part? This might imply that they are attempting to subdue you by their physical dominance. The ability to interpret body language in dangerous circumstances can help you defend yourself or, at the least, be prepared in the event of a violent incident.

Using body language may also be a way for you to rescue someone else from an unpleasant or hazardous circumstance. For those of us who have been there, we know how difficult it can be to speak out or just walk away when confronted with a potentially dangerous or unpleasant situation, owing to social norms in the former case and frequently the prospect of physical damage in the latter. There are times when a bystander's ability to understand body language might save a person's life. This is something I can attest to from personal experience.

When it comes down to it, successfully communicating and delivering the proper message to others depends on your ability to recognise and comprehend your body language and conduct. All languages, including body language, convey meaning to others.

4

How confident women speak

REGARDLESS OF WHAT we want to change inside ourselves, we must first peel back the layers of our past to set a firm foundation for the future we want to build for ourselves.

Some individuals like to go to the source of their problems, while others prefer to start from scratch, with a blank slate to deal with. Despite our desire to leap right into being more forceful, our foundations entail learning how to cope with our uncertainties and concerns.

When we think about being bold, we're more likely to feel apprehensive or anxious. Fear and anxiety are not the same, even though they have similar characteristics.

When we're afraid, we focus on a more precise threat rather than being tied to a particular thing or circumstance. Because it's tied to something particular, worry may turn into terror. If you're feeling anxious, it may be because you're experiencing other sensations like mental conflict or shyness. When we are afraid, our impulse to fight or flee activates.

Many individuals are afraid of speaking in front of a large audience, but this is merely a concept, and there is no real risk. Standing on a stage, prepared to address an audience, is a terrifying experience. Deep breathing, for example, is a common strategy for coping with anxiety and fear. It will be discussed in this chapter how we deal with our fears and anxieties while working on our self-confidence.

Being confident can bring up several concerns.

No, we're not going to assume that we all have the same fears. Fears that we're about to talk about could resonate with certain folks. It's also entirely acceptable to be afraid of assertiveness for whatever reason. Asserting oneself may cause a wide range of anxieties, including:

This fear may include but is not limited to concern that the other person will turn physically aggressive when enraged. The fact that you feel this way does not imply that you have a history of anger or violence. The individual with whom you must be forceful may have previously engaged in hostile conduct.

Fear of an angry reaction isn't everything. The other person in the discussion will not accept a no is also a little frightening. To avoid having to back down or attempt to impose ourselves again because the other person won't accept no for an answer, we are afraid to say no.

You may be afraid of disappointing the other person. What I remember most about my childhood is when my parents were angry with me, I sulked for a while, but nothing hurt more than when my parents stated they were disappointed in me. The expression of disappointment might be enough to cause a person to become paralysed in fear of certain people.

Not being pleasant might be daunting if you have people-pleasing characteristics. It's easily mistaken to say no for being rude or hurtful to others, even if we don't intend it. Because being a kind person is a virtue, this is a difficult obstacle to overcome. Instead of worrying about being cruel, you can comfort in knowing that you may be assertive while still being kind.

There may be a fear of being embarrassed or humiliated in social circumstances. It's common for us to doubt the validity of our convictions and thoughts. The topic may shift to the next election or new medical research. You've done your research, but you're afraid to speak out if others make fun of what you have to say.

We must learn to deal with our fear of being rejected to go through life. When we're in high school, this is a common occurrence. There is a strong desire to fit in and be accepted by others in the early years. Toward the close of these key years, we discover more about ourselves and the people we want to maintain in our lives. It's easier to cope when you're excluded from particular social circles. The dread of being rejected is ingrained in people pleasers and nonassertive because of our compulsion to be liked.

Because we are in danger, we find ourselves in various scenarios. Confidence is required at this point. If you're ready to start talking and your legs start shaking, and your face starts losing colour, you may be nervous.

Why do we feel anxious being confident?

The thought of being forceful causes us anxiety. It might begin days or even weeks before a critical discussion. Some individuals are paralysed by fear of circumstances in which they will have to be forceful. This is not to say that this feeling is unfounded or should be discounted as a figment of our imaginations. The circumstance isn't there, contrary to popular belief.

Worrying about having to return food that you haven't even ordered is an example of being nervous. When the anxiety turns into fear, you are worried that you will have to throw out the food.

As a general rule, every scenario or incident that might lead us to feel fearful will also make us anxious. Anxiety, according to psychologists, is a fear-based condition. A constant worry about what might happen is exhausting, and this is why it can lead to a host of other health problems.

Being confident when you're afraid.

When you start to feel the onset of fear, it's important to focus on the following:

- Fears are something that everyone experiences. One of our most basic instincts is fear, which helps us survive and protect ourselves. You can either rationalise your fears or accept them as a normal part of life. The most important thing is to learn how not to be overcome by your fears rather than focusing on how to overcome your fears.
- Assert yourself without fear by using visualisation techniques. You can use visualisation to train your brain to think more positively. Visualise yourself overcoming your anxieties with total confidence. Pay attention to the other senses you can conjure up. You're teaching your brain a new way of thinking by reciting this visual image repeatedly.
- As soon as possible, confront your fear of assertiveness. Don't stop responding to your boss's request if you know you need to do so. Without it, your anxiety will only get worse.
- Consider the worst-case situation if possible. It may seem counterintuitive, but thinking about the worst-case scenario might help you put things into perspective. Any unfavourable response is a sign that the other individual does not have good communication skills. The worst-case scenario for you is that you'll have to keep working on your project. Even if your anxieties are valid, the severity of the problem may be exaggerated.
- Keep your goals in mind, and don't lose sight of them. Imagine what you'll be doing instead of working overtime if you have to decline. Have you been anticipating your next workout or romantic dinner with your partner? Instead of dwelling on the negative aspects of the circumstance, pay attention to the good.

And last, the most important one:

- Confront your anxiety. This is the most difficult aspect of the process, and I've found that knowing a little bit about the science behind it helps a lot. Exposure to fear has been proven to change neural activity over time. A mild shock was administered to the mice in the box. They froze in fear the second time they were placed in the box. It took some time for the mice to become used to being in the box again without being shocked. We've all been there. When we begin to confront our fears, it gets easier.

The key is to get started. When you follow the first five pieces of advice, you'll start to see the effects of number six.

Learning how to manage anxiety.

One of the greatest methods to learn how to handle anxiety is to make tiny lifestyle changes since it happens more often and continuously. Making a daily schedule may help alleviate anxiety, which often arises from worrying about the future. When you know what's coming up in your day, you're better able to deal with stress. In terms of routine, you should have the following two components:

1. Consistent dietary intake. As our blood sugar levels drop and our stress hormone cortisol is released, skipping meals is a bad idea. Anxious people will feel worse if they have a little cortisol in their system, which is excellent since it may help them perform better under stress.

2. Get some sleep. Without sleep, our anxiety levels rise. Anxiety may make it difficult to get a good night's sleep, but developing a soothing nighttime routine might help. Avoid coffee, stick to a regular bedtime, and swap your electronic gadget for a book.

Other ways to properly deal with anxiety and even minimise it include:

- Increase your body's serotonin levels and endorphins by doing some exercise. You'll be able to focus better when you have more oxygen in your blood. It doesn't have to be a gruelling session at the gym to get the benefits of physical activity. A quick stroll in the woods, a dance party, or a yoga class are excellent options. There are many Exergames (video games that are exercise), and I can fit them into my morning routine, whether it's 10 minutes or an hour.

- Reduce your intake of caffeinated beverages to a minimum. Caffeine may cause anxiety episodes by raising the heart rate. Begin by cutting down on your caffeinated beverages and looking into alternate options. Anxiety may be eased by drinking water, green tea, and Valerian root tea.

- Be aware of what causes you to react in a certain way. When being assertive, individuals' anxiousness will be aroused by many things and people in particular, much as their worries. I've even discovered that particular odours and melodies might make me anxious. When you can, try to get rid of the things causing you anxiety. If a co-worker is causing you anxiety, avoid them unless it is for business purposes.

- Make a shift in what you're doing. Take a deep breath and allow yourself to relax when you begin to feel anxious. Change your activities after a brief time of acknowledging your feelings. Take a break from your workstation if you've been sitting there for a while. Switch to music if you are watching the news.

- Try to keep your brain active. Choose an activity that stimulates the brain if a change in activities is not enough. If you don't do anything to occupy your mind as worry starts to grow, it might overthink and contribute to the bad sensations.

- Consume brain-stimulating foods to keep your mind engaged. Doodling is fine, but drawing is better. Keep a few 'brain games on your phone for mental stimulation. Several apps might help you relax, such as Sudoku,

Prune (a horticulture game), and Headspace (a mindfulness and meditation app).

- Reducing anxiety by changing your routines will help you focus on other things.

Cognitive distortions caused by negative beliefs

Our poor and negative sentiments are reinforced by the awful and negative experiences when attempting to be aggressive.

As long as we don't allow these sensations to become a permanent part of our identity, we may learn from all of our negative emotions. "I've never been able to assert myself, so I won't." The following are steps we can take to avoid falling into this trap.

- Identify the ideas that cause you to feel anxious.
- Take a step back, step back from the issue, and look at the facts from all aspects and interpretations.
- You would talk to your friends; you should also talk to yourself. There's nothing wrong with telling yourself that you won't perform well on a test, but don't do it to your friends.
- Make sure your ideas make sense to others before you put them into action. Social settings and meeting new people might benefit greatly from this when you want to seem forceful and are afraid it will backfire. Friends and family members may share their experiences in new social environments.
- Reattribution. After a bad event, instead of blaming ourselves for it, reattribution is about looking at the circumstance and determining who or what else was responsible for it. It's not the same as pointing the finger at others; it's about accepting responsibility.
- The benefits and drawbacks of your negative attitude. Writing a list of the benefits and drawbacks of feeling this way can provide you with a visual representation of how your ideas have influenced your actions.

- Keep an eye out for any clairvoyant tendencies. I work with many people who would never consider seeing a fortune teller. Despite this, people believe they can negatively predict the future. Reading minds and making educated guesses about what someone is thinking are examples of this phenomenon.
- Stay away from selective abstractions. When we think back on our past, we tend to focus on the unpleasant aspects instead of the good ones. When assessing your past efforts at assertiveness, seek a bright spot in each one. You may have tried a tactic that doesn't work for you, or you may have found a new barrier that you aren't comfortable with.

How to become a master of your own mind

There are many ways to define your inner game, but essentially, it's the struggle you have with yourself, your anxieties, and your doubts. It's all about how you feel about yourself and your self-esteem.

Your inner game may apply to every element of your life, from romance to job to riches and more, but the way we play our inner game in terms of assertiveness matters most now.

Our inner game has four elements: take control, employ "I" words, make things simple, and not compromise.

Take charge of your life.

The message you wish to convey should be yours, not someone else's. Think about what you want to say and how you want to express it. If you're going to tell someone that you're upset because they don't respect your no, think about what words you will use. Make a plan for how and when to say what you need to say.

Ultimately, the message you want to convey is yours to own, so you determine what to say and when. Taking control of our life becomes possible as we become more assertive.

Statements that begin with "I" statements are preferable.

It's impossible to overestimate the power of "I" statements. To show people that you are responsible for your emotions, use "I" statements. It demonstrates that you have a strong opinion on a certain topic while also reducing the risk that your comment will be interpreted as a personal attack. Both of these phrases have a similar meaning, but the message's recipient may perceive them differently. You're blaming the other person for your feelings of weakness by saying, "You don't listen to me." When we take responsibility for our feelings, we say, "I feel weak when you don't listen to me."

Maintain simplicity and be straightforward.

You know how it's tough to stop if you keep talking, particularly if you're nervous? It's easy to forget your initial point with so many different words and thoughts floating about. There is a problem with the way you've conveyed your message. It also allows the other person time to come up with an answer to your no. As an illustration of how to be concise and straightforward, consider the following:

- "No, thank you."
- "Later I'm busy."
- "I'm not in the mood."
- "That is not good for me."
- Don't begin with a compromise.

The other person will know there is wiggle space if you start with a compromise. Assuming there is no response, they'll presume that the answer is yes. After your message, compromise is a wonderful approach to ensure that things get done, and issues get handled.

5

Take a break - What's been holding you back?

WE TEND to think of self-awareness as just another set of abilities that we all possess. It shouldn't be that tough to perceive ourselves as we are right now. However, given the complexity of the human mind and the many levels of self-awareness, it is logical that some direction is necessary.

We are conscious of our thoughts and emotions while going about our everyday routines. The things that we like or dislike are clear to us. We've figured out what sets off our anxieties and concerns. However, we don't consider whether or not these ideas are accurate.

Being self-aware is having an awareness of your own emotions and ideas so that you can examine them to see whether they're in line with your ideals. In this self-evaluation, we need to be objective and compare ourselves to our standards rather than merely identifying our feelings.

Recognising and accepting one's strengths and weaknesses may lead to more self-acceptance, self-confidence, better judgment, and more effective communication. Enhance your experiences by being able to assess yourself in a variety of scenarios objectively. Instead of delving into how to cultivate self-awareness, let's look at how assertiveness affects our other feelings.

Criticism and negative feedback

According to Winston Churchill, Criticism is an essential experience for us to learn and develop. When we've been attacked for our beliefs, it's positive because we've shown that we're willing to stand up for them. Even though you had high hopes for the project you presented, being criticised or given negative feedback can leave you feeling hurt, angry, or incompetent.

Critics have a myriad of reasons for their opinions to be negative. That doesn't mean they aren't trying to assist, but they just don't communicate well.

As a result, they may feel as if you haven't listened to them thoroughly enough. They may have made their errors and attempted to distract attention away from them by bringing attention to yours. Of course, it might also be because they're afraid of you or insecure or afraid of what you could do to them.

To respond assertively to unfavourable comments and criticism, you must first maintain your composure and take a deep breath. Accept just what you believe to be accurate from the critique. Dispute the person's false claims. A person's tone of voice is not as essential as what they say. You may think they're being aggressive or upset, but you can't match their volume. Don't become emotionally involved with them. Consider delaying further discussion until you've had a chance to analyse the input and determine how to react if you've had your self-esteem shaken or your feelings injured.

Negative thoughts

A positive outlook is essential, regardless of whether your negative ideas result from cognitive distortion or a predisposition to focus on the bad aspects of life. To be assertive, you must have a strong sense of self-confidence and the ability to express yourself clearly via body language and tone of voice. It is typically the idea that you can do something that gives you the self-confidence to execute it.

It's discouraging to hear when you're told that you need to be more upbeat. You are aware of this, but it is never that easy. It requires retraining the brain, which some people can achieve on their own, while others need the assistance of cognitive behavioural therapy (CBT).

When an opposing idea is identified, it is analysed to see whether it is genuine before being replaced with a more positive one:

The negative opinion: Your employer will be furious if you refuse to present this weekend.

Validating the opinion: Your employer may be upset, but he can't fire you or make you work on your day off. If they can yell, it'll be over soon enough.

The excellent view: You have dinner and drinks with friends that you will be able to enjoy without the burden of working on a Saturday.

It may seem simple, but it will take some time to hang it. It's critical that you take your time and don't hurry through each step for it to become ingrained in your routine.

Anger

Angry people have two sides to their personalities. We must first learn how to deal with individuals being angry when we express ourselves. This is a terrible circumstance, but you must not allow that to prevent you from being assertive. It will terrify the hell out of you, but we've figured out how to deal with our fears now.

Angry retaliation is the most critical thing to avoid. As a general rule, we tend to be passive individuals. In addition, this individual has passed an unacceptable line, and you should not enable them to believe that they may act in this manner.

When expressing your disapproval, use "I" expressions such as, "I don't appreciate being addressed to in this way." Then you may talk about it afterwards.

The best way to avoid an angry reaction from a person is to make sure other people are around when you speak out. This will keep things from spiralling out of control. While you're honing your assertiveness and aware that people get furious, think about utilising email or another electronic means of contact instead. In the written word, you may still make your point.

In contrast, folks who don't respect our desires when we express them might cause us to get irritated and frustrated. We must deal with our anger to prevent it from rotting and taking out on someone else.

There are several good strategies to cope with anger, such as the following:

- Begin counting backwards from ten and pay attention to your breathing. Put soothing images in your head to help you relax.
- Identify the feeling that is causing you to get angry. Was it because you felt embarrassed or threatened?
- Focus on your anger in your mind. Imagine it as an entirely other creature from yourself rather than attempting to shut it out.
- Find a way to express your rage physically, such as walking, playing an instrument, or creating art.
- Use relaxation techniques such as mindfulness and meditation to help you relax and de-stress.
- Refrain from adding to the gloom. It's possible that your employer was not the only one he yelled at that day. A sense of relief may come from participating, but it may also increase your feelings of dissatisfaction.
- Be kind to the angry individual. I know it's difficult, but you can do it! It doesn't matter if they're rude to you since you can still be your regular pleasant self. When you are nice to them, their conduct towards you will alter.
- Delaying your answer is always the wisest course of action when you feel angry. You will have a better chance of succeeding when you can keep your emotions under control since you will have had more time to consider things through. Remember the Marshmallow Challenge. The child who could hold off on eating the marshmallow was rewarded with two more. It was a challenge, but it paid off in the long run.

Overthinking

Overthinking is equally as dangerous as "cognitive distortion," which lacks a compelling psychological label. Our thoughts may be taken over by overthinking, making it impossible to concentrate on anything else—overthinking causes you to question yourself and reduces your self-esteem.

Ruminating and worrying are two forms of overthinking. Reliving an incident over and over in your mind, thinking about what you might have done better, is known as ruminating. As a result, you may blame yourself for the repercussions of your actions or inactions.

When you're worried, you're engaging in cognitive distortion. When we worry about the worst-case scenario, we're doing just that: anticipating the worst.

You should be able to break the loop of overthinking by engaging your brain in a new task. The elastic band trick is one of my personal favourites. Put on an elastic wrist band. Flick the band when you realise you're overanalysing things; it won't hurt, and it won't be a penalty. "Thoughts are not facts," say aloud. This is a technique for retraining our brains.

An excellent approach is to set a time limit on how much time you may spend making choices. Begin by making the simplest decisions. For instance, what to eat for dinner. Allow yourself five minutes to decide what to eat instead of overthinking it. This tells your brain that you only have a limited time to consider.

It could be good to have a few Post-It notes on hand. A Post-It that reads, "Am I overthinking?" might serve as a helpful reminder while determining what to eat, as does a similar one that asks, "Am I overthinking?"

It's time to examine your social circle. Do you prefer to associate with overly analytical folks or those who have a knack for putting things in perspective? To learn from them, spend more time with the second group.

A sense of guilt

People-pleasers have a hard time saying no without feeling bad. Being selfish makes us feel guilty, which leads to more selfish behaviour. You won't be free of your sense of shame if you do a magic trick. Making other people happy comes down to being a kind person.

Remember that guilt is a powerful motivator when it comes to assertiveness. Having a sense of wrongdoing is what causes us to feel guilty. Neither being forceful nor prioritising your own needs is bad. In other words, you should do what seems right to you. You don't have to feel bad about saying no to anything because you need to care for yourself. This is a legitimate option for you, as it is for everyone else.

Make sure your boundaries are in place before avoiding guilt. Set your standards for what is and isn't acceptable conduct for yourself. If you don't feel comfortable with your buddy making fun of your food, let them know how you feel. I don't know whether they knew that their insults had offended you. It's easier to establish oneself if they've been aware of your boundaries.

Controlling your emotions

Our emotions may go out of control if we don't handle them properly. As a result, we might easily succumb to our negative emotions, such as anger or pride, if we do not have them.

Emotional self-control requires focusing on the here and now rather than the past and how things ended.

Keeping your thoughts focused on the feelings you're experiencing in the here and now stops you from drifting into a state of "autopilot," which ties you to the past.

A good rule of thumb is to avoid categorising your feelings as "good" or "bad." Not everything can be reduced to a simple binary. As a result of naming emotions, we may label the scenario the same.

Every scenario contains a combination of feelings that we may learn from if we can look at the larger picture.

A quick surge of emotion may be very useful if you take a

moment to calm yourself. We tend to be much too hard on ourselves when we experience an overwhelming rush of emotions.

Stepping back gives us a moment of clarity and prevents us from acting on irrational emotions.

Taking a step back from our emotions and seeing ourselves as we do in self-awareness is an important part of emotional control.

How to become self-aware and control your emotions.

- Make time and space for yourself.

In our everyday lives, there is a continual level of tension. Our minds are always working no matter what time of day or night. It will never happen if we don't take the time to be aware of our thoughts, feelings, and emotions.

Even if it's only a few minutes a day, find a time each day when you can be alone and connect with yourself.

- Develop your mindfulness skills.

Your inner self and your reactions to people and events may be better understood via mindfulness. Instead of allowing your thoughts to wander from the past to the present, stay focused on the here and now.

Your breathing and any other senses you may be able to pick up on can help you relax. It's simple to include mindfulness into your routine since you can do it while walking or even eating.

- Seek feedback.

Those that care about you will be able to tell you exactly what you're thinking and feeling, even if you don't realise it yourself. As a result of talking to people, you'll get a new perspective on things and the ability to learn and grow, which will boost your self-confidence.

- Keep in a diary.

Journaling is a great technique to sort through your feelings and ideas. It might be difficult for some individuals to communicate their thoughts and feelings to others freely; therefore, keeping a notebook allows you to do so without fear of judgment.

- Pay attention to others.

Listening to others and seeing how others interact can teach you what to do and what not to do. Body language, speech, and expressions will all be visible as well. You don't have to judge how other people communicate; all you have to do is observe.

6

Daily routines for a confident woman

DECIDING to be more assertive and speak up for our values frequently prompts us to reflect on our inner state of being. Of course, we'll have to work on our self-esteem and interpersonal abilities. Nonetheless, there are ways in which we might make the procedure more convenient. We might refer to these as the physical or more concrete improvements that we want to see in addition to the emotional changes that we are hoping to experience.

Identifying and addressing your desires

If you don't know your needs, it will be tough for you to establish yourself. Your needs can be both bodily and emotional at the same time. Your relationship may lack respect or affection, and you may need to work on it. Some individuals need physical touch, such as a hug or a handshake, to experience that love.

Only until we can identify precisely what we require can we satisfy those needs. Each need has an associated or resulting sensation, and it is necessary to keep going back to the need to uncover the associated or resulting feeling. The "onion peeling technique" refers to the method we remove the outermost layers until we reach the root of our problems. When your expectations and desires are satisfied, how do you feel? First, I'm overwhelmed by the number of things I need to do before everyone returns home. Then I have a burst of energy and can do whatever I set out to achieve. I've created a massive wave of calm and serenity to wrap up my metaphorical onion. Now that I've pinpointed what I'm lacking, I can go on.

You must set aside time and space for the development of your requirements. It's going to be the most difficult portion since you'll constantly feel like someone or something needs this time more than you do. Every excuse you make not to give yourself a break is like a baseball hurtling at you at full speed. Don't give up until you have no more excuses left to give.

Goal-setting

It doesn't matter whether you name their goals, dreams, heart's wishes, bucket list, or anything else—there are so many terms for what we want to accomplish. We want to accomplish big things like purchasing a home or travelling across the world in the long run. Objectives over the following six to twelve months will include progressing up the professional ladder and short-term goals. It is still a goal for those of us who keep a daily to-do list.

The ability to set and achieve goals is essential for everyone, as they serve as a source of inspiration and drive for a hard effort. They assist us in growing as individuals by encouraging us to study and grow. They provide us with a reason to be thankful.

Becoming more self-assured may help you achieve your objectives. Breaking this into smaller stages, our first objective would be to inform someone that you'd consider it, rather than saying no outright. We may begin by cutting down on fatty meals before embarking on the kale smoothies and one-hour spinning classes. There are several ways that you may save money for an Australian vacation, such as putting aside money for flights, lodging, and other expenses.

The next stage is to create a strategy for achieving your minor goals. For example, if our goal was to lose weight, we might accomplish our first step by giving up sweets and chocolate in the first week, followed by fried meals in the second week, and so on.

It is necessary to jot down every one of your objectives and the measures necessary to get there. Sharing your objectives with as many people as possible is also a good idea. When you make them real, you are held responsible. If John woke up one morning and decided to paint his living room, but he didn't write it down or notify his wife, his desire is not documentation. No one needs to know if he fails. In telling his wife, he would have the added benefit of having her support him the rest of the day and be able to mark everything off his list that he had completed successfully.

How to improve your habits

These are just a few of the behaviours that a person who isn't aggressive may have:

- They do not call out socially inappropriate conduct such as queuing, coming late, or speaking with your mouth full.
- Nobody will start a discussion with them.
- When requested to participate in a discussion, they will likely agree with the majority rather than express their own views.
- They are afraid of seeming stupid if they ask questions.
- They are capable of emotional deception.
- They have a hard time accepting compliments.
- They may have a weak or quiet voice.
- They will find it difficult to look each other in the eyes.
- Nervous behaviours like nail-biting, hair-pulling, and pen-clicking are common among them.
- When they do smile, it's more of an awkward grin than a real one.

Make a list of five or six of your bad behaviours. Find out what's causing these bad behaviours. Prepare an action plan for when these bad behaviours reappear in your life. One habit at a time, focus on one change at a time. Changing too many things at once is not something you should force yourself to do.

Changing the way you see the world.

Connecting the linkages between your environment and your capacity to exert yourself is not probable unless you do. It is important to have self-confidence and self-esteem to be more forceful. If you want to be happy, you need to take care of your happiness, love yourself, and be thankful for what you have.

Compile a wish list of home improvement projects you'd want to do. Your house may benefit from a thorough spring cleaning, or you may want to start painting and redesigning to feel more positive about your surroundings. If your full-time work isn't fulfilling you, you may want to consider upgrading your resume before looking for another one.

It's also important to think about the individuals you're surrounding yourself with. There are certain individuals in your life who intentionally or unintentionally make you feel horrible about yourself. Some may find it difficult to accept the adjustments you'd want to make in your life.

Avoid these individuals as much as possible, and do your best to shield yourself and your surroundings from their negativity. In the beginning, these folks might hurt your growth. That's not to mean that you should fully get rid of them from your life. As you gain strength and self-assurance in your capacity to stand up for yourself, you may put some distance between yourself and the other person.

How to identify your boundaries

Boundaries, like needs, may be difficult to identify. Most people don't recognise they have a boundary until they cross it since they don't know how they feel until they are in the circumstance in question. It's important to figure out what you can't do.

When it comes to social media, the following limitations may be taken into account:

- Although I like having a social media account, I don't use it.
- People may talk about me on their social media profiles without my permission.
- People uploading images of me on social media are off-limits for me.
- When you see a picture of yourself online, it's possible that you won't realise how violated you feel. You can't be furious at the one who posted it because the person who posted it has no idea how you feel.

It's hard to grow a comprehensive list of what constitutes acceptable behaviour since everyone's choices are unique. You may investigate the following five types of boundaries:

1. Physical boundaries: your own body, your personal space.
2. Feeling your emotions is an important part of establishing emotional boundaries.
3. What is acceptable and what is not acceptable in terms of sexual boundaries
4. Intellectual boundaries: tolerance for differing viewpoints, ideas, and values.
5. It is important to know when to lend and when it is appropriate not to lend money.

It's a good idea to reflect on the last year or two events to see what has disturbed, hurt or enraged you. Someone may have crossed a line, but you haven't given it a name. Do not overlook the need to establish clear boundaries in your personal and professional interactions.

Remember that Rome wasn't built in a day, and we don't have to accomplish everything at once before you start writing down all the behaviours and practices you want to modify. Look at what you can do this week, this month, and in the following three months after you've finished the list. To see long-term results, it's best to put in as much work as possible upfront.

Up to this point, we've put in a lot of time and effort to create life-enriching adjustments that we're proud of. It is clear that we are getting more confident and have a clear idea of our goals. It's time to put everything you've learned into practice and be more confident.

7

How confident women act

WOMEN HAVE ALWAYS HAD to put in a lot of effort, even if they weren't rewarded for it. When it comes to taking on the responsibilities of raising a family or maintaining a household, women always could get their hands dirty. As women, we've demonstrated many times that we can achieve everything we put our minds to. Women work as directors, administrators, artists, authors, servers, teachers, academics, garbage collectors, monarchs, executives, activists, etc. What you need is out there, and a lady can get it done.

Success means different things to different people. We are confident in our skills, and we will not allow anybody to convince us differently. Moreover, what do you know? You're also excellent at what you do. Regardless of how long you've been doing your work or how much you've learned along the way, you can rest certain that you are a skilled professional doing an excellent job. What you do at your best is what your employers require, not what you do at your best because it's good enough for them. You're a one-of-a-kind individual.

The only thing that matters right now is whether or not you believe you'll be here for the next five months or five years. It's up to you to make it happen. If success means becoming the CEO of a Fortune 500 business before you retire, do whatever it takes to get there—and do it without treading on the reluctant backs of others. Take pleasure in your job as a mother if it means raising children who grow up to be remarkable people. You simply have to find out how you're going to accomplish it if making a difference means changing the world for the better. And don't worry if you haven't figured out what success means to you just yet. A stance you don't detest is the first step toward figuring it out later.

The bottom line is that you can accomplish whatever you desire (though I might advise against anything with questionable legality, myself). Your concept of success will alter as you grow and evolve. Whatever you choose to accomplish with your profession, you should be confident in your abilities and believe that nothing is impossible for you. You can and will accomplish your objectives. When you look in the mirror each morning, take the time to confirm your abilities and the certain success that awaits you.

Examples of successful women

Michelle Obama

Besides being the 44th First Lady of the United States, Michelle Obama is an American lawyer, writer, and the creator of Let's Move!, an effort to combat childhood obesity. She is also an advocate for the rights of women and LGBT people and a supporter of education reform.

Michelle Robinson was born in 1964 in Chicago. Following graduating from Princeton in 1985, she went on to get a law degree from Harvard Law School in 1988, after which she worked as a corporate attorney at Sidley Austin, a well-known Chicago law firm. In 1989, Sidley invited Michelle to supervise a summer associate named Barack Obama, despite the firm's policy of not accepting first-year law students as associates. After finishing his time as an associate, he returned to Harvard, and they married in 1992 after a long-distance romance. Also, at the same time, Michelle considered her options in the business law field during this period. Instead of staying at Sidley Austin, she moved to work for the City of Chicago, first for Mayor Richard M. Daley and subsequently for Planning and Development Director Valerie Jarrett. During her time in that post, she worked tirelessly to create jobs and revitalise Chicago's communities, and she never looked back.

The First Lady of the United States, Michelle Obama, worked in hospital management at the University of Chicago Hospitals until her husband's election victory in 2008. While serving in this capacity, she was an outspoken supporter of military families, working mothers who had to combine job and family, and the arts. Michelle and her husband worked together to pass the Employment Non-Discrimination Act and repeal Don't Ask, Don't Tell, two landmark pieces of anti-LGBT legislation. In 2010, she started the "Let's Move" initiative to fight child obesity and establish a healthy lifestyle for American children.

Indira Gandhi

The life of Indira Nehru Gandhi, India's first female prime minister, reflects the country's divisions. In honour of Mahatma Gandhi, her husband, Feroze Jehangir Ghandy, an activist, publisher, and politician, adopted the last name "Gandhi." Indian independence came to fruition under the stewardship of Gandhi and her family members as a young child. Gandhi's visit with the Nehrus in 1919 prompted the rich family to give up their things and join the fight for freedom. Indira also formed the adolescent revolutionaries' The Monkey Brigade, and she was brutally assaulted for marching with India's flag. Gandhi was "always there in my life; he had a tremendous effect on my growth," and she and her family visited him often.

India's Congress Party welcomed Indira into its fold after Gandhi's death and sustained violence throughout the Partition, which divided India's Hindu majority from its Muslim majority. In 1947, her father became Prime Minister of India, and he required Indira to serve as his official hostess since he was a widower. Indira stepped into the shoes of the Prime Minister when her father was battling numerous strokes. The Congress Party elected her as its leader in 1966 following the death of her father's successor. She had served in

India's upper chamber of parliament since her father's death in 1964. With it, she became the first female prime minister in a nation where women's rights were not a high priority. She became an inspiration to millions of Indian women, who had historically been subordinate to men.

Indira inherited a country plagued by famine, civil conflict, hyperinflation, and religious uprisings. To satisfy the requirements of the world's second-largest population, she put her health at risk by working 16-hour days. During her tenure as Prime Minister, her political fortunes soared and fell; in 1977, she was forced from office only to be re-elected to a fourth term a few years later. Amidst accusations that she paid political favours to keep her job, her birth control program is largely neglected.

The history of Indira Gandhi's cabinet is a laundry list of riots, upheavals, and revolutions, all playing out on political quicksand. Her murder clearly showed this in 1984. Sikhs throughout India, including some of Gandhi's bodyguards, blamed her for the country's ills. A Sikh assassin killed Indira in her garden four months later.

So, what does it mean to you to be successful? Use one of those sticky notes that you probably took out while reading the introduction to jot down your thoughts on this. You could, of course, post it right here. Writing it down in a place where it's easy to find is a good idea, but make sure you look at it often. Even if you're not moving ahead or backwards in the direction, you desire, having a clear picture of your end goal in front of your face is a great way to keep yourself on track.

Confident statements for different situations

To begin, let's focus on saying no when appropriate. Every one of the statements we'll examine has something to do with being asked to do something we don't want to do. Your answer is likely to be greeted with a resounding yes. As time went on, folks were so used to me responding yes that they didn't even bother to wait for a response.

Empathy and understanding are the primary goals of this series of simple no-statements. Therefore we preface each with a "Thank you." Using some of the lengthier forceful remarks will help you enhance your capacity for empathy.

- "Thank you, but I don't have the time."
- "Thank you, but I have other things on my mind."
- "Thank you, but I'm not interested."
- "The gesture is appreciated, but I'll have to decline your offer."
- "Thank you for informing me, but I will not be able to attend."
- "Thanks for considering me, but I'm fully occupied at the moment."

In the next paragraphs, you will be given extra time to determine whether or not to act. Or, if you're prepared to say no, you'll be able to do it more confidently.

- "There is so much in my thoughts that I need some time to review everything."
- "Permit me to mull it over for a while."
- "I'm not certain; I'll get back to you."
- "I'll think about it when I complete this work."
- "I can get back to you later tomorrow/later if you'd like?"

To convey our feelings or ideas, we employ "I" sentences. It's best to avoid using the personal pronoun "you" in the first word of your sentence.

- "I see your point of view, but I disagree."
- "I feel disrespected when you interrupt me/laugh at my opinions/or ignore me."
- "I take offence to what you've stated."
- "I'd appreciate it if you'd allow me to express my thoughts."
- "I'm not a fan of getting yelled at like that."

- "Your tone of voice/language is making me uneasy."

Building up to more strong comments that incorporate the word no. You may keep it brief and to the point or soften it up a little if you wish.

- "No."
- "Certainly not."
- "No, thank you."
- "No, not today."
- "Thanks, but no thanks."
- "That's not the issue. I've got another commitment."
- "No, it is not possible today."

It has been said before, but it bears repeating: you have the right to make any of these bold claims. Tell yourself that you're doing nothing wrong as long as you don't come off as aggressive in the process.

Confident body language.

Experts and psychologists may differ on this point. Faking it till you make it is a common adage. Although you may not feel confident, you can project that confidence by focusing on your body language. Others assert that your body language will automatically reflect your increased self-assurance as you gain greater consciousness. I advise individuals to work on both since both are possible.

During a forceful talk, you may begin to lose some of your self-confidence. It's amazing how changing your body language may still make you look confident. However, body language alone is insufficient. We can't become more self-aware until we first have a sense of self-assurance. We'll examine forceful body language not as a replacement for our confidence but rather as a supplement.

Don't slouch your shoulders; feel confident.

It's best to keep your hands out of sight. Putting your hands behind your back suggests that you're concealing something from the world around you. Using open hands indicates that you are willing to share your thoughts and feelings.

Maintain a direct look at the speaker at all times.

Maintain a level of eye contact that is comfortable for you.

Take care not to look about the room hurriedly. It's a sign that you're worried.

Do not shout, but speak loud enough to be heard clearly.

Do not fumble with your words. Speak slowly and steadily.

Maintain a calm demeanour and a genuine grin at all times.

Your body language and how these minor adjustments are perceived may be improved by practising in front of a mirror. It's also a good idea to work on your body language with a buddy you can trust.

Learning to be confident in our relationships

Even before we contemplate being assertive in our interactions, we experience various emotions. No matter how annoying they might be, our significant others can't exist without us, and our families can be loved or hated in equal measure.

We don't want to harm or disappoint these individuals in our lives. Their well-being and happiness are more important than anybody else's.

In personal relationships, asserting ourselves maybe a little simpler since we have a greater sense of self-confidence with them.

However, our need to win their approval might further confuse matters.

There are simple steps you may take to begin defending your rights. Let's begin with a look at our relationships.

Being confident with your friends.

There are two sorts of friendships to consider: long-term relationships with people you've known for a long time and more recent ones. The new acquaintances you've made are the best individuals with which to practice becoming more assertive. When the initial discomfort wears off, you're confident in your decision to pursue a relationship with this person. The problem is that they don't know you very well.

You need to start again with a clean slate when you meet new people. Your lack of assertiveness or difficulty saying no is unknown to them.

This will make it easy for you to set boundaries with your new buddies. Make it clear that you don't expect them to do this for you. Your friends and family may start doing the same once they see how clear-cut your boundaries are.

We have a beautiful, honest, and open relationship because of this. Much if you already have a solid relationship, you may discover that it's even better because of this. After all, to them, you're not doing anything unusual.

There are some actions you can take to assist you in first identifying where the issue is coming from so that you can then work toward the answers in long-term friendships.

1. Examine your friendships.

You may be under the impression that your input isn't being considered. It might be that you're always checking up on the other person or feeling like you're being left out of the discussion. You and the other person possibly make plans together, but the other person continuously cancels on you.

Consider circumstances in which you have been disappointed by your pals. What triggered your emotions?

2. Keep a record of your emotions.

You'll be able to keep track of the many situations when asserting yourself is appropriate. Patterns in the relationship will become apparent, and you must break them.

It will also allow you to deal with your emotions and thoughts. Understand not just why you're hurting but also when and why it happened.

Keep a diary to come up with solutions to your challenges.

3. Share your feelings with your pals.

Asserting yourself doesn't have to be seen as bullying, even when it is. You'll become stressed out if you build it up to a large discussion.

Instead, have a casual conversation over a cup of coffee or a bottle of wine. Describe how you've been feeling and what you want to see happen.

Find strategies to strengthen your connection with your partner.

You and your partner may be able to join up for a new activity together, more in line with your interests than your very own.

4. Be assertive if the conduct you don't like persists.

Once you have had the first talk, it will be easier. You've previously addressed this with your pal, so you're good to go. When talking with pals, maintain your composure and utilise stronger adjectives to convey your feelings. Instead of angry, you might use furious.

5. If your buddy continues to neglect you, it may be time to reevaluate your friendship.

Even though it seems difficult, it is doubtful that they will alter their minds once you have properly conveyed your thoughts. Keep in mind that ignoring you indicates passive-aggressive conduct, which is their issue, not yours.

6. Think about making new friends.

It's possible to meet new people when you're separating yourself from buddies that don't appreciate you. If you're looking for a new hobby, try a new sports class or anything else that interests you. Here, you could meet folks with similar interests as yours.

When a buddy cares about you, he or she will do everything in their power to set things right. There's no need to worry that you'll soon be alone. It's not always possible for even the finest friendships to last for long periods.

Consider if staying alone with this individual and feeling miserable is preferable to making new friends.

This isn't nearly as simple when it comes to family.

When your family doesn't appreciate your confidence.

The chances are that you are not the only one who has miscommunicated with your loved ones. There's a good chance you've felt like you've been walked over while you've been inactive. You may have screamed and felt terrible afterwards in a moment of wrath.

Taking a more proactive stance with your family offers several advantages, both for you and them. It's a great way to de-escalate stressful situations.

Both parties can express themselves quietly instead of feeling irritated and expressing negative emotions. This improves communication. A deeper understanding of one's sentiments and those of others is gained by all those who participate.

At least, in the beginning, being assertive with your family is more about having good communication than exerting yourself. Here are some ideas for improving family communication.

Try to avoid comparing yourself to others.

Your children's self-esteem and confidence might be lowered if you compare them to other family members. To assert one's originality, it is necessary to acknowledge that being unique has its advantages and disadvantages.

Show that you have a good grasp of the subject matter.

If you want to be able to stand up for yourself, you need to show respect for others.

Try to comprehend the sentiments of your family members and express empathy for them. Listen to each other's feelings and try to understand what they are going through.

What you're expressing should be very clear. "Would you want to go out for dinner?" is an example of a question that asks what you believe others want to do. The idea indicates that you'd want to go out to dinner, but it's not obvious what that means. Instead, you should say, "I'd like to go out to dinner." You shouldn't be dismayed if a family member expresses an interest in joining you.

Do not waffle. When we start talking too much, we seem insecure, and our confidence loses its effectiveness. Keep in mind some of the short, precise, forceful remarks that we've rehearsed and strive hard to adhere to.

Be honest with your loved ones.

Often, your body will tell you what you're not saying. While your words may convey one set of emotions, your body language is a more accurate reflection of your true feelings.

Your message will be muddled if you tell white lies to avoid hurting someone else's emotions.

What should you do if your family ignores your assertiveness?

We're dealing with parents who don't value our independence or appreciate our right to make our own choices most of the time. "Toxic Love" is what we call it. They may seem to be treating us as if we were still children and not trusting us to make our own decisions. This may be upsetting since, as accomplished adults, they should be able to put their faith in your judgment by now. The difficulty is that when others question your decisions or viewpoints, you begin to doubt yourself and feel bad about it.

To better our communication skills, we've studied the topic of empathising with the sentiments of others. Even if you've been frustrated in the past by your parents' constant supervision, it's important to remember how your parents are feeling as well. Parents may attempt to influence you occasionally, as we'll go into a moment. However, most of the time, it's simply fear on your parents' part. You can see why a parent might desire to shield their adult kid from harm or errors. They may also be afraid of being left behind as you go farther away from home. The older they become, the more they think they need you and want to keep you near. This may seem silly if you're in your 30s or 40s.

Empathy kicks in when you view your parents as terrified instead of overpowering, making it easier to communicate with them.

You may show them that you've thought through every stage of your decision-making process by explaining how you arrived at your conclusions. They'll realise that you didn't simply choose anything at random when you've made sure you've thought about every possible scenario.

A strong hand is required for manipulation. A manipulative person may still feel some fear, but it's inexcusable because they've considered your assertiveness and used guilt and shame to obtain what they want instead of asserting themselves. These people are good at making you feel uncaring about them. It doesn't matter who the offending member of your family is; the first thing you should do is calm yourself and get away from the situation.

Take a step back and look at the big picture. Their manipulation methods may be motivated by self-interest and selfishness. There's a chance they simply want to spend some time with you, but they're going about it the incorrect way. You'll be better able to reply if you understand how they manipulate you.

To better understand their desire, get them to provide additional details. Before you agree to assist your father, be sure to figure out exactly what he needs from you. A modest work request might signify that he only wants to see you or that your mother has bribed him. You may determine whether or not to assist him if he needs it.

Using "I" statements to convey your emotions without disrespecting people might help you recognise when you're being influenced. "I don't enjoy it when I'm forced to do something that I don't want to."

Do not tolerate interruptions. "In addition to demonstrating a lack of regard for your emotions, failing to let you complete a statement and interrupting you are also symptoms of disrespect. To avoid a pot calling the kettle black situation, avoid interrupting them to inform them that you don't appreciate being interrupted. "Please don't interrupt me" should be enough to make your message clear to the other person.

Your family member should appreciate you more now that you could explain yourself, and they listened and took everything on board. Although helpful, a forceful reminder like "Mum, we spoke about how it feels when you tell me to do something," should not need a display of assertiveness that causes you to feel uncomfortable or afraid.

Sadly, there will be moments when others continue to disregard your presence. It's more difficult to put space between yourself and your adversaries than with your friends. If you desire a meaningful connection with your family, you must stand up for yourself.

Take a hard look in the mirror and be honest with yourself. Because you haven't done anything wrong, you have no reason to feel furious with yourself. It is important, though, to remind yourself that you have established limits with your family members. You've reminded them of the rules, yet they're still ignoring you despite it. Your confidence in getting what you want will become stronger if you are tough on yourself.

The only way to stop family members from forcing you to do things you don't want to do is to make forceful remarks or simply say no.

Assertiveness is a virtue, not a failure. Remind yourself of this. Because of this person's lack of regard, you must be assertive. An example of an ultra-assertive statement is the simple "no."

"Stop!"

"That's enough."

"I'm not going to stand for this."

"I said no, and I mean no."

"I'm not interested in making plans with you again because of your lack of regard for others."

"I can't respect you when you behave like this."

Ultra-assertiveness is not aggressive, even if it's very assertive. Your bluntness may annoy the other person. Let them know that you'll be back when they calm down and walk away. You should be pleased with the progress you've made and the superb communication skills you've developed.

Enabling Your Partner to See Your Confident Side.

When two people are inseparable like this, they are both family and friends. Because you spend more time with your partner than with your friends and family, you can't avoid becoming pushy. And you can't give up on your relationship if you don't feel that your partner values your thoughts or wants.

Since we've previously spoken about these methods with our friends and family, this is why we need to employ a mix of them all. Let's summarise the assertive actions that may be employed in relationships without going over the same ground again.

Ensure that your communication is built on a firm basis.

Don't hold back your emotions for fear of upsetting your family. It's preferable that you and your partner can talk about your feelings as soon as they occur than to wait until things get out of hand.

Explain to your spouse that you don't like it when they leave their dirty dishes all over the place and that both of you have a responsibility to keep the house in order.

Listen to what they have to say.

Recognise and appreciate their viewpoint. A real mistake should be handled if the phone rang and they forgot. If you keep bringing up the dirty dishes, you're implying that you haven't paid attention to what the other person has said.

Accept responsibility for your actions and inactions.

Understandably, there will be times when you fail to tidy up after yourself when doing the dishes. Tick-tocking isn't a helpful response when someone says, "Well, you left your laundry on the floor."

Be courteous.

It may seem elementary, but we tend to get complacent and even expect the worst, so we stop saying please and thank you. Healthy communication includes expressing thanks.

Be fair to one another.

Even though we live in the 21st century, this is still a major problem for many couples. It's not just about who performs the chores; it's about how everyone is treated. Equalise your resources, including money and time, and your freedom to express your views. Relationship equality can only be achieved via compromise and discussion.

Never compromise or apologise for your values or beliefs.

Having the same values and views isn't a must for being in a relationship. Regardless of what you think, each of you must be loyal to yourself and respect the opinions of others around you.

When asserting yourself, avoid making your partner feel as though they are to blame by focusing on remarks explaining how you feel rather than blaming them. Rather than saying, "You're making me feel," use phrases like "I feel" or "You've made me feel."

Dissociate your emotions from your goals.

It's one thing to be conscious of your feelings, but another to let those feelings distort your judgment. Instead of attempting to demonstrate your anger, your goal here is to let them know you're upset about something.

Do not be afraid to be assertive, even if it means going beyond.

We may be afraid of the other person's response if we are assertive, but we are afraid that this person will leave us more often than not. One of three things may happen when you are forceful in a relationship:
1. Your partner learns to accept your values, boundaries, and points of view.
2. The scenario may lead to an argument, which is not always negative. Controversy is pleasant because it forces you to confront your feelings.

3. Your relationship may fail, not because you expressed yourself, but because your personality types were not in sync.

If you look at it this way, it may seem harsh, but there will be a wide range of degrees of each following: When you are far from the worst-case situation, try not to dwell on the worst-case scenario. Becoming more assertive in your relationship doesn't need getting into an argument. It's just a way to get your point through. When individuals in various relationships have differing perspectives, there's nothing wrong with that. If everyone thought and did the same thing, life would be very boring. Instead of arguing about differences, learn from them and broaden your horizons.

8

Confident women in the workplace

WORKPLACE RELATIONSHIPS MAY BE as difficult. Many of us have worked with co-workers that we consider friends, while others we'd like to avoid at all costs. When it comes to our employers, there are some that we fear and those who we want to impress. Non-assertive people have much more obstacles when they're in charge.

Our co-workers aren't our friends, but it doesn't give us the right to be passive participants in our job. There are few things more important than being able to express yourself freely at work without worrying about the implications, especially when you're there for so many hours each week.

Our tendency as employees is to put forth extra effort to be the hard-working, dependable person our bosses want. Isn't this dedication that will bring us to the promotion we want? No, I don't think so.

If you don't have the confidence to say no in the office, you'll find yourself doing the work that no one else wants to perform. A co-worker who doesn't want to be put in the position will seek you for help. You'll be asked to cover for someone who doesn't want to be on call over the weekend. To avoid burnout, we need to be able to say no to these extra activities without affecting our productivity.

In addition, saying yes to everyone at work will eat away at your free time.

Your personal and professional interactions need similar levels of confidence. Assertiveness at work is about expressing yourself courteously and confidently so that you and your co-workers get the treatment you deserve. It is possible to create individual and team objectives, but you don't need to be pushy about them, and you may say no if required. All of this may be accomplished while still fostering excellent working relationships.

Asserting yourself as a worker

Making your presence known at work requires mastering the following principles, which we've already discussed:

- Increasing your self-confidence and self-esteem. Think about what you do well and what you're excellent at.
- Stepping back to have a better perspective on the situation.
- Decide whether you wish to respond yes or no to the question.
- The best way to get your point across is to write it down in a few simple phrases.
- You may use "I" statements to express your thoughts and emotions more clearly.
- Maintaining eye contact, standing up straight, and smiling are examples of body language that you should pay attention to.
- Rather than saying yes under duress, ask for more time if you aren't sure.
- When you assert yourself, be firm. Let your responses speak for themselves, and don't feel the need to defend them.

In contrast to other relationships, each employee is entitled to specific rights in the workplace. There are limits to what can be done legally and ethically. Legal limits may also be crossed, or law may be breached if you find yourself in a situation where one of your boundaries has been violated. It's not only women who are subjected to sexual advances; guys are just as guilty. Some people may consider a pat on the back or a shoulder massage to constitute sexual harassment, while others may not. It's unethical for a worker to approach you and ask for a $20 loan from the register. Here are some guidelines to keep in mind when working:

- Using language that isn't appropriate.
- Abuse of language.
- Sexual contact.
- Sexual advances.
- The act of revealing one's personal details.
- Disclosing private information.
- Accepting client gifts.
- Disobeying religious or cultural norms or practices.

You should get familiar with your job's legal and ethical limits so that you are better equipped to claim your rights if your boundaries are being violated.

Also, review your contract to determine your specific legal obligations and rights. There's a good chance your employer is breaking the law if he or she asks you to work through your lunch hour. As long as you have the support of the law, it doesn't seem like you're fighting alone. Your employee policy handbook has all of the information you need.

If you still have trouble standing up for yourself in the job, consider the possibility that you aren't the only one being exploited. Many people will find themselves in the same predicament as you if you continue this pattern of behaviour.

There are a lot of issues that aren't your fault, but the sense of accomplishment you'd get from standing up for yourself and righting a wrong would do wonders for your self-esteem and how others see you.

Asserting yourself as a boss

As a young woman in her twenties, Olivia hired a guy in his late fifties. Generally speaking, they had a pleasant working relationship. Regardless of how uncomfortable it made him, she silently accepted that he would never be happy working for a woman as his boss.

A few weeks later, he requested her to assist him with personal administration, was nasty to a customer, and didn't show up to two meetings without even warning her. He felt angry when she emphasised that this conduct was unacceptable. At that moment, she realised she'd have to be creative.

The following day, when things had settled down, she asked him to her home (it wasn't the first time, and they had previously enjoyed social situations, so she thought it wasn't wrong). Inquiring about his well-being, she offered him a drink. The guy wept and claimed he felt he would get a harsh punishment. They discussed everything that had occurred and settled all difficulties.

Employer-employee relationships would be damaged if this practice were widely adopted. In short, bosses may exert themselves in various ways without making their staff uncomfortable or seeming to be the bad guy.

Choosing your fights is a wise strategy.

It's your job as a team leader to keep an eye on your group's performance, not everyone else's. A manager or director's assertions should be directed at the team's leaders. You shouldn't micromanage everyone but rather concentrate on the most pressing issues.

Clarify your goals for the project.

Your expectations, like limits, encompass what you can and can't accept. Displaying, talking about, and teaching these standards should all be part of the hiring process. When someone doesn't live up to your standards, it's simpler to exert your authority and resolve the problem.

Encourage inquiries.

To foster good communication, you should encourage your team members and/or team leaders to ask questions. As a result, fewer mistakes are made since employees feel more comfortable asking for clarification if they don't comprehend the instructions.

Your workers' body language should mirror your own.

No, if they're all lifelessly slumped around the table. Instead of standing or pacing around the table, sit down with them if they are already seated. This might be an indication of dominance or hostile conduct.

Learn to say no.

People think that saying no to a request is a simple matter for a manager. It's not uncommon for bosses to be people-pleasers who want the admiration and respect of their subordinates. The request for an employee to work an hour later than usual may appear insignificant at first. Your workers are suddenly flooding you with daily demands for changes to their work schedules.

Make an honest evaluation of each request to see whether it is feasible and will not negatively affect the rest of the company's operations. Accept those that share your viewpoint.

Make it clear to your staff that you'll get back to them as quickly as possible if you're uncertain.

If you can't come to a choice, ask for additional information.

Show empathy for those who don't agree with you. The staff should be thanked for their efforts. If their suggestion doesn't work now, let them know that you'll keep it in mind for future consideration.

As a precaution, examine your body language and make required modifications, such as sitting up straighter. "Thank you, but I've previously answered your request," for example.

The only area in which employers can afford to be passive is when it comes to enforcing their own legal and ethical standards. If somebody comes to you with a problem, it must be dealt with right away, no matter how little it may seem. Even though it may make you feel uncomfortable, you will succeed if you use the communication skills you've mastered. The prospect of being sued for failing to deal with the problem is more stressful and expensive than having a single assertive dialogue.

Being assertive in the workplace is an effective communication strategy that may aid in the resolution of disputes, improve teamwork, and raise employee satisfaction. Disagreements in viewpoints are anticipated when so many diverse personalities are working together in close quarters. Here's the last tip to help you become more forceful at work. Suggest assertiveness training to your employer or team leaders!

Knowing when and how to speak up for yourself

Throughout the day, you will be faced with several opportunities to determine whether or not to defend your interests. You fear that you'll be known as a constantly unpleasant person and think it's best to shut your mouth.

You start a conversation and then get all agitated, and then you feel like an idiot. As a result, there are those occasions when you regret not standing up for yourself. There's nothing worse than replaying a discussion in your brain and wondering, "If only I had said that," or "Why didn't I think of it at the time?"

We've already discussed the significance of being confident to establish oneself. When you know when to speak up for yourself, you'll have a greater sense of self-confidence.

In this section, you'll discover when it's OK to speak out and defend your ideas and convictions and when it's best to wait.

Regardless of your surroundings or the people around you, there are times when you must defend your interests. Violence, sexual assaults, and verbal and physical abuse cannot be ignored. Long-term consequences may result from ignoring these concerns. Let the other person know precisely how you feel and that their conduct is unacceptable.

You can understand if you lack the courage to speak out at the time since even the most forceful persons might be taken off their feet by such infractions.

The problem must, however, be addressed with the cooperation of others. Talk to your boss or the police if you have a problem at work. Let a buddy join you at the train station if that's what you need to do.

Take these easy steps to help you make a better judgment in those times when you aren't sure:

- First and foremost, is this the right time?
- Take a look at how you two are feeling right now. Have you had a difficult day, or are you just simply tired? No matter how long the discussion is, interruptions are a fact of life.
- Are you certain that the other person will pay attention to what you say?
- Can you see how easily distracted they will be? As far as I can tell, I don't believe that they're in the correct mindset. The moment may not be appropriate, or they may not be able to listen to you in the future.
- Is your emotional state stable?
- If you're not controlling your emotions, it may be best to wait. You must be able to convey your point without becoming enraged or irritated.
- Determine what has made you angry, irritated, or upset.
- Be specific about why you feel this way so that the other person understands why you are feeling this way.
- Could you be more confident at another time?
- We feel more confident when we have a better understanding of a problem. Do you believe that you could learn more about this circumstance and deal with it later when you have more information and confidence?
- Consider whether there is space for flexibility.
- You've been asked to do something, and you're not eager to comply. You have a different viewpoint than the one expressed by the other individual. Is it possible to find an

alternative, a common ground, or a solution? There may be a better moment to talk if you don't know yet.

How to defend yourself

You must be steadfast and persistent after you have decided to stand up for yourself. We've studied and prepared for this moment, and you've chosen your words carefully and are paying attention to how you're expressing yourself physically.

Count to five or ten if you need to take a few deep breaths so that you don't come out as too pushy. You can boost your self-esteem and posture naturally by increasing the amount of oxygen in your brain and body.

Don't feel obligated to apologise to anybody. As we've seen, there are many ways to be assertive. It's important to pick one that's comfortable for you. It may or may not contain a thank you or apologies. Ultimately, it's up to you to decide.

Change the topic or end the discussion. No one expects the exchange to go on for an extended period. Longer conversations increase your vulnerability to being persuaded otherwise or using coercive tactics. Remember that any talk that makes you feel uncomfortable is not because you have done anything wrong. Defending your interests is well within your rights.

It's also crucial to remember that you may not do it correctly the first time. This, however, does not constitute a mistake. Practising a new skill is essential to mastering it. You may conclude that you're either passive or aggressive in certain situations. This is where we will focus our attention next: achieving a healthy equilibrium.

The following are some more suggestions to help you boldly stand up for yourself in the face of adversity:

- You need to figure out what is upsetting you. You may begin to ramble on about topics that only you understand. People won't know what you think if you don't say anything. Start by determining what is causing you to have a hard time.
- Avoid allowing people to dictate how you feel. In certain

situations, not even your closest friends know how you feel. Do not let others tell you that your tiredness is because you stayed up too late. Only you know why you're weary or even whether you are.
- Consider the viewpoint of the other person. However, it is still possible to stand up for yourself while still showing compassion for others around you. Many difficulties may be solved by looking at things from various angles and perspectives. It also improves your emotional intelligence.
- Keep calm and go on in the face of the oncoming storm. Sticking up for ourselves may seem to conflict with this, but it all comes down to deciding which fights to take on. You should use the methods listed above to defend yourself if you find yourself the target of a verbal assault. There is no purpose in engaging in conversation with those with no regard for you. Ride it out and wait until they've cooled down before reaching out to them by email or text message.
- If you want to be appreciated, treat the other person with respect. This implies paying attention, not yelling, and respecting others' boundaries. The importance of respect cannot be overstated.
- Don't let the task at hand go undone. You've done your best to defend yourself when you've spoken what you need to say. Avoid leaving with the impression that you still have something to say. If this continues, the problem will only become worse.

9

Understanding how to manage different types of treatment from others

IF ONLY WE could express ourselves confidently, knowing that the other person would just answer, "Okay." If we didn't have to worry about being singled out by our employer if we said no to him, life would be a lot simpler, right? For example, it would be nice to be able to tell our parents we don't want to spend Christmas with them and not feel guilty about it.

There are no guarantees in life, and we must be ready to deal with whatever kind of treatment we may get, from being told no to crying and insults.

Even though I've mentioned it before, it bears repeating since it's so critical to your success that you speak up for yourself.

It's not a bad idea to say "no" or express your viewpoint. When you speak out for yourself, you take back control of your emotions. Accept that asserting oneself is not only acceptable but also beneficial.

Learn to deal with the guilt and fear of saying no using our mastered skills. However, you can't control the other person's emotions. Accept that the issue is out of your control while being calm and confident. Both parties are necessary for effective communication to take place.

Let's look at how others could react to us when we're more confident.

Dealing with aggression

When someone gets hostile, we tend to blame ourselves, as if we were to blame for their anger. Their reaction was negative. When someone feels threatened, they are more likely to become aggressive. The strain of assertiveness may be felt by your supervisor, for example, who has become used to having their way with you and would now have to find someone else for all of the things you put up with doing. Some of your close pals may be concerned that they won't be able to have the same influence on you as before. Fear may be the source of their hostility, but they cannot communicate it, so they get enraged. In no way am I saying that we're making excuses for them, but it's always helpful to consider things from their point of view.

To avoid unwittingly becoming more menacing, it's important to understand that the violence stems from a sensation of being threatened.

Make alterations to your posture and facial expressions. So that the other person understands you aren't afraid, be open and make appropriate amounts of eye contact.

To avoid jerky motions, slow down your pace. You can't calm yourself down by furiously waving your arms. Make a conscious effort to avoid interfering with a person's privacy.

Regardless of what the other person does, it is important to be courteous. It demonstrates that you are courteous and will not respond to anger with anger.

Listen to what the other person has to say and your thoughts and feelings. Keep the conversation focused on the good aspects of the situation rather than the criticisms that were made.

Sayings like "You need to calm down" or "You can't talk to me like that" will only worsen the situation. While both of these statements are correct, you should stick to strong "I" statements like "I don't like being shouted at in this way" instead.

If they become furious, don't say yes simply because you want to be kind. There is no way for them to learn to appreciate your aggressiveness. Say no as calmly as you can until they accept your refusal.

Return to the subject when they have calmed down if they refuse to accept your no or your opinion.

Think about your experience. If you want to process what occurred, write about it or speak to a friend. Working through your emotions can help you avoid repeating the scenario in your thoughts or losing sleep over it.

Stop telling yourself, "They were simply having a terrible day." No one should take their angst out on others, even when they have a difficult day.

You mustn't minimise the toll that violent conduct has had on your life. Legal or ethical violations should be reported regardless of personal or professional.

The aim is to calm things down, which will require some self-control. Even while it's quite improbable that you'll attack back, you also need to have enough self-control not to flee the scenario entirely.

How to manage manipulation

The truth is that no one is flawless, and most individuals can recall a moment when they used manipulation to achieve what they wanted. That final bit of chocolate has brought out the puppy eyes, and the bottom lip has dropped. We'll get through this. We're talking about those who are adept at identifying your flaws and using them for their own gain. Because the Parent-Teacher Association (PTA) is aware that you can't say no to making 200 cupcakes for the bake sale and responds with remarks like "but nobody bakes cupcakes like you," you're unable to say no to them.

If you have just returned from holiday and your supervisor wants you to work extra, it would be unfair for them to condemn you for saying no since you have just returned from a relaxing vacation. All sorts of manipulation, including lying, neglecting, and misleading others, are examples of this. It's not what they expected. Therefore they're using your weaknesses to achieve what they want. Passive-aggressive behaviour is still manipulation if your partner fails to clean the floors correctly, knowing that you will have to repeat it. A tougher hand is needed for manipulative persons.

As a first step, be more confident in saying no. Empathy or other solutions are not necessary.

Manipulative people want to play the victim and make you believe that you are to blame for everything that goes wrong. To avoid offending the person who should be taking responsibility for your actions, refrain from apologising.

Let the insults fall off your back. To elicit a response from you, they hurl insults and condemnation your way. They're curious to see how far they can push the buttons. You become the theatrical one if you respond emotionally. Walk away and tell them it's a pity they feel that way.

Be confident in your intuition. Manipulators may use doubt to exert control. There is a nefarious motive behind their actions. You know exactly what you want in your heart, and you've given it some serious consideration before making a choice. Don't let them make you question your abilities.

Don't worry about what other people think of you. Fear of losing or the desire for an immediate solution is unneeded stress. When a salesman tells you that the product you're interested in won't be available in the future, they're trying to get you to buy now. There aren't many non-urgent issues that need to be addressed right now.

If someone is being manipulative, don't attempt to change them. This will not change them, even if you voice your displeasure and say that you will no longer accept it. We can, at most, prevent them from mistreating you in the future.

The more passive-aggressive or manipulative someone is, the less time I have for them. They believe they're wiser than everyone else, but it's actually because they don't know how to communicate effectively. They don't have a good sense of empathy. Despite your best efforts, some may still attempt to manipulate you. In these situations, the best course of action is to maintain a safe distance from the manipulator. Many wonderful individuals are out there who will treat you with respect and dignity. Don't be fooled by manipulators —even if they attempt to convince you otherwise!

What to do when people make fun of you for being firm

You are not being shamed for your assertiveness in the same way we were earlier in the book. Confidence in your own morality is a more powerful motivator than guilt.

Imagine you confronted a co-worker about their approach and made it clear that you didn't agree with it. Because you used your freedom to voice your viewpoint courteously and fairly, there is no need to feel guilty or shameful. If your co-worker turns around and publicly humiliates you by calling you an idiot, they have humiliated you. As a result of your distress and humiliation, you may not be able to reply. Instead, your face flushes, and you wish the earth could suck you up. Here's how to deal with those that put you down for standing up for yourself.

Keep a cool head, and don't overreact. It's good that your body is under shock, including your tongue and brain. When the brain isn't ready to respond, it hinders you from responding at the moment. You risk more humiliation if you don't take a minute to comprehend the issue properly.

You haven't done anything wrong. Therefore there's no need to apologise. To avoid more bullying, avoid apologising for things that aren't your fault.

The person's shame may have been an effort at constructive criticism that failed. Even while this isn't an excuse, it will benefit you in the future.

As soon as the event is complete, inquire about a suitable time to meet privately with the individual you were speaking with.

Make it clear to the other person that your treatment was unacceptable and that it isn't essential. In my perspective, constructive criticism is appreciated, but I don't enjoy being humiliated for speaking my mind. It's possible that they didn't plan to offend you in the first place.

Make it clear to the individual that you prefer that they speak privately with you about any issues they are having rather than with the rest of the group. They can improve their communication skills by speaking to you one-on-one, rather than in front of a large group. When you and your partner are the only ones in the room, it will be much simpler to get the self-assurance you need to speak up for yourself.

Do not take any humiliation personally, and do not let it damage your self-esteem. You should be happy with your accomplishments since you accomplished everything correctly. To safeguard your self-esteem, focus on the good aspects of your life.

In my experience, you should only respond in the heat of the moment unless you are feeling confident. It's difficult to stand up for yourself when someone constantly disparages you. It might destroy all of the hard work you've put in. That doesn't mean the offender should be allowed to get away with his or her conduct. Again, the key is to assert yourself at the appropriate moment to be well-prepared and self-assured to deal with the circumstance.

Asserting yourself may cause a lot of stress, so here's how you handle it

Never fear. During this time, you'll be learning new abilities and experiencing some discomfort. Your worry and tension will diminish with time, making it easier to do the task. While you wait for this moment, you may use some stress-relieving tactics to help you be more assertive when the time comes.

Accept the challenge of being assertive.

Instead of seeing assertiveness as a source of stress, think of it as an opportunity to grow as a person by overcoming the difficulty. You'll gain emotional stamina by completing this task.

Recognise that there are things you can't change.

The woman in front of you will bypass the line because she is impatient and will think she is not being penalised. Your parking space is about to be taken by an arrogant motorist. You have no control over any of this.

People abusing their power or taking advantage of your good

nature shouldn't be a source of anxiety for you since their actions, not yours, are what matters.

Chew gum.

When I say "chew gum," I'm not implying that you should open your mouth wide so that everyone can hear every swish of your gum. That's more than enough to irritate any person. Chewing gum produces brain waves comparable to those of a calm person because it increases blood flow to the brain.

Laugh your tension away.

You'll take some time to gather your thoughts and figure out what you want to say before speaking up. While you're waiting for your turn to speak, amuse yourself by watching a funny movie online. Relaxing your muscles and relieving stress are two benefits of laughing that may help you improve your body language.

Put an end to your procrastination.

The choice is between saying no or saying yes. You've already decided to take charge of your psyche. There is a risk of escalating the stress level by debating the issue anymore. Even a few days after this, your health will begin to suffer.

Take a few deep breaths.

Aside from providing your brain and body with the oxygen they need, deep breaths may also help you relax and bring about a sensation of tranquillity.

Conclusion

We've spent too many centuries ignoring what's directly in front of us and what's over our heads. We have lost this most fundamental biofeedback system due to a puritanical mindset and the mechanical assumption of "I think, therefore I am." You'll be linked up to a machine that monitors your physiological responses for biofeedback.

Your decision to read this book has enabled you to take your best qualities and make them even greater. To better understand yourself and the people in your life, you'll have improved your communication abilities. You may be able to view others in a new way after studying the value of empathy. If your mother begs to see you all the time, she isn't attempting to take over your life. She may simply be lonely. By spending time identifying her interests and activities, you not only ensure her happiness but also free up your time to pursue other interests of your own. Your ability to articulate your feelings and persuade others to see things from your perspective is invaluable when dealing with stubborn friends who refuse to do what you want.

Stress at work affects millions of people each year, and it is a very real phenomenon. We spend a large percentage of our waking hours at work. Therefore it's imperative that we like what we're doing. It's natural to have a terrible day at work now and again, but it begins to affect our free time and weekends when it happens regularly. We're thinking about it even though we aren't physically present. The first step in regaining some control over your professional life is establishing boundaries for when you are not at work. The greatest workers aren't always available, and no one can keep up a constant state of emergency response. Colleagues who take advantage of your generosity are selfish and unjust, which is not acceptable. When a manager cannot control their fury or thinks it's entertaining to humiliate you, they've crossed a line that they don't have the right to cross. But don't worry, you now have the power to end it.

I hope you've had as much fun reading this book as I did writing it. I have equipped you with the knowledge and skills necessary to go out there and express yourself and be confident in your day-to-day life, and I am certain that you can.

You're on the correct path into full confidence in your life, so keep your spirits up. You can do this.

Feedback

Thank you for reading 'What Confident Women Do.' I sincerely hope you enjoyed and got value from this book, and that it helps you to forge those all-important positive habits that will bring peace and harmony to your life from this moment on.

If you have a free moment, please leave me some feedback on Amazon.

Also, scan the QR code below to visit the Hackney and Jones Publishing website where you can find more information on the range of books available.

 HackneyandJones.com

www.ingramcontent.com/pod-product-compliance
Lightning Source LLC
Chambersburg PA
CBHW031546080526
44588CB00018B/2716